PRIDE & PREJUDICE

PRIDE & PREJUDICE

HEALING DIVISION IN THE MODERN FAMILY

DR. MATT R. SALMON

MANUSCRIPTS
PRESS

MANUSCRIPT PRESS
COPYRIGHT © 2024 DR. MATT R. SALMON
All rights reserved.

PRIDE & PREJUDICE
Healing Division in the Modern Family

ISBN   979-8-88926-102-5 *Paperback*
       979-8-88926-274-9 *Hardcover*
       979-8-88504-355-7 *eBook*

For Jimmy,
the best boy.

Contents

INTRODUCTION	**ANSWERING THE CALL**	**11**
PART 1.	**TRADITION**	**23**
CHAPTER 1.	FAMILY ASSIGNED AT BIRTH	25
CHAPTER 2.	THE GARDEN	37
CHAPTER 3.	PURSUIT OF HAPPINESS	49
PART 2.	**DIVISION**	**61**
CHAPTER 4.	MONOPOLY	63
CHAPTER 5.	NEUROFABULOUS	75
CHAPTER 6.	WRESTLE WITH MY SELF-LOATHING	87
CHAPTER 7.	CONVERTING TWO BY TWO	101
PART 3.	**EVOLUTION**	**115**
CHAPTER 8.	FINDING PARADISE	117
CHAPTER 9.	LOVE THY NEIGHBOR	131
CHAPTER 10.	RETURNING TO THE CAVE	145
CONCLUSION	**EMBRACING THE JOURNEY**	**159**
RESOURCES		**169**
ABOUT THE COVER ILLUSTRATION		**175**
ACKNOWLEDGMENTS		**177**
APPENDIX		**183**

Queer people don't grow up as ourselves, we grow up playing a version of ourselves that sacrifices authenticity to minimize humiliation and prejudice. The massive task of our adult lives is to unpick which parts of ourselves are truly us and which parts we've created to protect us. It's massive and existential and difficult. But I'm convinced that being confronted with the need for profound self-discovery so explicitly (and often early in life!) is a gift in disguise. We come out the other end wiser and truer to ourselves.

—ALEXANDER LEON

Introduction

Answering the Call

In the spring of 2013, my dad was newly reelected to the US House of Representatives, serving Arizona's 5th District. During a live interview, the reporter asked if his opinion about same-gender marriage had changed, since I am queer and was publicly out and loud about it for a few years by then.

I was in my third year of medical school and recently decided I'd become a child, adolescent, and adult psychiatrist. The psychological trauma I suffered at the hands of a licensed professional counselor (LPC) in my youth through so-called *conversion therapy* fueled my ambition.

At that time, multiple prominent Republicans, like Senator Rob Portman and Representative Liz Cheney, changed their own stances on marriage equality after learning one of their loved ones was LGBTQ+.

"We were surprised to learn [our son] is gay but knew he was still the same person he'd always been," Senator Portman explained about his evolution. "The only difference was that now we had a more complete picture of the son we love... The overriding message of love and compassion that I take from the Bible, and certainly the Golden Rule, and the fact I believe our maker created us all, that has all influenced me in terms of my change on this issue... It allowed me to think of this issue from a new perspective, and that's of a dad who loves his son a lot and wants him to have the same opportunities that his brother and sister would have."[1]

That day, I learned from a Google alert my dad had not changed his opinion. He told the journalist how much he loves me, but I shouldn't be granted the right to marry a man I'd love.

"I don't support gay marriage," my dad told the reporter. "My son is by far one of the most important people in my life. I love him more than I can say. I'm just not there as far as believing in my heart that we should change 2,000 years of social policy in favor of a redefinition of the family. I'm not there. It doesn't mean I don't have respect. It doesn't mean I don't sympathize with some of the issues. It just means I haven't evolved to that station."[2]

The story became national news, and I found myself pulled into the media storm. Several outlets, including CNN's *Piers Morgan Live* and MSNBC's *The Last Word with Lawrence O'Donnell*, reached out to me for comments and to interview me about his position.

I expressed willingness to participate, but while I neither condoned nor endorsed his beliefs and correlated actions, I would not speak out against him. Instead, I informed them I would offer my forgiveness and understanding. I was surprised, given how enthusiastic they originally seemed, when the shows decided not to book me for the interviews.

I suppose a lack of controversy isn't good for ratings.

One evening later, my friend Travis and I wandered Safeway looking for some snacks and wine for our movie night. While we did, we discussed my recent experiences and how I would tell my story, given the chance.

"How wild would it be if Anderson Cooper wanted to interview me?" I fantasized over my celebrity crush, shivering a bit from the cold of the ice cream aisle under the bright, fluorescent lights.

Not moments later, while in the checkout line with a basket containing pints of ice cream and bottles of wine, I received a call from a New York area code.

"Hi, Matt. My name is Elisa. I'm a producer for *Anderson Cooper 360 (AC360)* on CNN. Anderson Cooper heard your story. He would like to have you on the show." I was grateful when Elisa assured me they were not interested in pitting me against my dad.

"It would be my honor," I replied. It was a no-brainer, really.

Three days later, Travis and I were on a flight to New York City.

While on *AC360*, Anderson wondered how I could maintain love and support for my parents. "I mean, you publicly said you have a loving relationship with your dad, a very close relationship. You feel he respects you, and yet he does not believe you should have the same marriage rights that he has. How do you reconcile that?"

"I decided that no matter what our differences in opinion are, we just have to love and support each other," I responded.

Anderson then asked me about my experience with sexual orientation conversion efforts, or conversion therapy, which I stopped about five years prior.

I couldn't help but sit there, starstruck. He was kind, but it still took much of my energy not to tremble nervously. My dad warned me about *gotcha* journalists who would try to manipulate me into saying something controversial, but that was not my experience.

I told Anderson I felt fortunate because the LPC challenged me to face certain insecurities I carried, which he claimed contributed to my sexuality. The LPC and I spent a fair amount of time role-playing to increase my confidence in talking to men.

"The goal," he said, "is to replenish the deficit of healthy male bonding that triggered your sexual attraction. Your mind made the exotic erotic."

I recounted these experiences live on *AC360* that night, and Anderson stopped me in disbelief.

"I think your doctor probably right now is spitting up his coffee," he exclaimed. "So, going through reparative therapy made you more confident in meeting guys?"

The bright lights washed out all onlookers, but I was keenly aware of their presence. Anderson sat across from me in awe, and something clicked for me.

I convinced myself I was fortunate. However, *I* turned my trauma into a purpose. I *made* it mean something. I dug deep and found a light that could only diminish if I allowed it. A light I kept bright with my passion for change and growth.

After the interview, Elisa approached me. She thanked me, told me I was a natural, and asked if I had any interest in being on television. I couldn't believe what I was hearing. I kick myself at times thinking about it, but I knew I would regret not finishing my education and psychiatric training. I had the determination to grow my knowledge and experience before targeting the ideologies woven into the fabric of our society, which contribute to the harms experienced by others like me.

The next Saturday, my dad asked to spend the day together. While we drove out to a large expo in Scottsdale, Arizona, he said my interview with Anderson was the push he needed to evolve.

"Matt, I hope you know how proud I am of you for always fighting for what you believe in, especially when we don't agree," he told me while keeping his eyes on the road. "You know how Anderson asked you if I would be at your wedding? I told your mother that night, while we watched the interview, I will be there, and I hope she will too. If she chooses not to go, I will go without her. I love your mother so much, and I hope you can experience the joys of love and marriage like us."

With that, I knew I was on the right path. Others belittled my experience and choices, but I would never regret choosing to accept my family, even before they accepted me.

I would never regret deciding love matters more.

So What?

We live in an era of growing division and tribalism stemming from a fear of those we consider different. My family is an example of one divided by conflicting beliefs that grew in understanding and empathy for one another, which enabled us to celebrate each other. The *us versus them* mentality we started with lacks love, acceptance, and understanding.

Individuals and communities grow more inflexible in their attitudes toward one another. I want to tell you how to grow together and move forward from a place of common ground and bridge building.

In ancient times, *othering*—the tendency to view anyone considered different as an outsider—may have been an "adaptive behavioral response... by promoting behavior in which organisms place their personal or inclusive fitness above those of other organisms."[4] By excluding others due to generalizations made about them or by forcing them to conform, tribes could shield themselves from new diseases, loss of resources, violence, et cetera.

While othering may have been adaptive for survival in ancient times, today, we recognize it is detrimental to the progress of our species. Humans evolved intellectually and socially, with a greater capacity to challenge biases, and developed better ways to protect ourselves from health-related threats.[5]

Despite great advancement, we cling to archaic beliefs that significantly harm millions of marginalized people—those who face discrimination and reduced access to basic needs.

We cannot ignore the impact of countless systemic inequities. Certain socially driven factors, intricately woven into our societies and systems of government, cause individuals from minority groups persistent and pervasive stress in their lives.

These factors are the social determinants of health: socioeconomic status, education, employment, housing, neighborhood and environment, social support networks, access to healthcare, and exposure to violence *or discrimination*.

The World Health Organization (WHO) reports, "The social determinants can be more important than health care or lifestyle choices in influencing health. For example, numerous studies suggest [they] account for between 30–55 percent of health outcomes. Addressing [them] appropriately is fundamental for improving health and reducing long-standing inequities in health, which requires action by all sectors and civil society."[6]

Been There; Done That

As a queer kid growing up in a super conservative, Mormon bubble, I recognized my community and society did not tolerate my identity. From a young age, my church and community taught me being queer was an abomination. My family's and my religious beliefs contributed to our inability to embrace my sexual identity.

After I accepted myself, I recognized religion indoctrinated my family for decades not to question church authority. I had to trust their misguided beliefs did not prohibit them from loving me. In fact, their love for me is why they experienced such great turmoil.

They allowed fear to guide them rather than lean into love. I decided to take the high road and extend them grace while I nurtured their evolution toward the celebration of diversity in all its forms.

Today, I look back and see the immense pain I experienced throughout my youth sparked the empathy that allowed me to understand and forgive my family. My journey led me to become a psychiatrist because I wanted to help others in similar positions prevent and heal from the harm.

My lived experience gives me a singular lens for viewing reality. However, through my work, I regularly get to peer through others' lenses and grow my capacity to see the reality of the world.

Why Read It?

As you read this book, I'll take you on a similar journey. Herein, I propose a moral evolution from intolerance of others' perceived differences to the celebration of diversity.

Tolerance and acceptance are not enough.

Nearly half of the United States still permits state-licensed professionals to subject minors to the damaging effects of Sexual Orientation and Gender Identity and Expression Change Efforts (SOGIECE), with some even prohibiting its ban on the grounds of religious freedom.[3] How psychological abuse of children is a religious right needing protection eludes me, but this is the world we live in. More and more, politicians feel they can legislate their religious beliefs despite evidence they are harming people.

I wrote this book because people are suffering at the hands of churches steeped in hypocrisy. This book isn't only for those with more conservative beliefs. Intolerance doesn't have a political party. It's not necessary to agree with or understand another's perspective to respect their boundaries and wishes, recognize everyone has immense value and potential, and grant all people equal access to "Life, Liberty and the pursuit of Happiness."[7]

It's time to evolve beyond the division and build bridges from common ground.

It's for You

This book is for anyone at odds with someone they love because of conflicting beliefs. It serves those who would rather grow together than apart. It's for anyone working to accept diverse experiences, who is willing to evolve their own perspective for the greater good. It offers hope and validation to the marginalized. It's for the conscientious, caring parent of an LGBTQ+ child who has misinformation about their child's identity and wants to avoid harming them.

This book is for anyone who feels uncomfortable with others having beliefs and practices that are different from theirs. It highlights the dangers of perpetuating the status quo and urges action by those who influence policy.

If the status quo has ever caused you or someone you care about harm, read this book, and let's do something about it. The sooner we accept our differences are our greatest strengths, to harness rather than extinguish, the sooner we can grow together and create a better society.

My family and I moved from a position of total opposition to one where we embraced our differences. Yours can too.

It's time for societal reformation—an evolution, if you will.

We all have to agree love matters more.

PART I
TRADITION

CHAPTER 1

Family Assigned at Birth

"You can choose your friends, but you sho' can't choose your family, an' they're still kin to you no matter whether you acknowledge 'em or not, and it makes you look right silly when you don't."[1] Atticus Finch's words from the 1960 classic *To Kill a Mockingbird*, by Pulitzer Prize-winning novelist Harper Lee, have significant relevance to this day—especially for LGBTQ+ individuals.

The families assigned to us at birth often reject us. If we don't find a chosen family, we'll be terribly alone. That's why I disagree with the claim that "it makes you look right silly when you don't" acknowledge your family. For the LGBTQ+ person, their family looks "right silly" for rejecting them.

I chose my family, and I'll tell you why.

My mom is the type who would take me, her enthusiastic sidekick, on spontaneous adventures while we ran errands together. One summer evening, driving around Mesa, our hometown, she spotted a blimp in the blue, orange, and pink sky of an Arizona sunset. Excitedly pointing to direct my attention, she exclaimed, "Let's follow it so we can watch it land!"

It didn't matter that we still had errands to run, including groceries to buy for dinner that night. In an instant, we set a new course, chasing the ship while it descended to the airfield like a balloon that lost its helium.

One of my earliest memories of feeling safe and cared for was bath time. My mom would sit on the edge of the tub while I splashed in the warm water. I'd laugh at how much it tickled when she brushed my teeth while I soaked. At the end, she would scoop me up in a ginormous, fluffy bath towel and hold me close while I sat on her lap and dried.

My dad was my liaison to the world beyond the religious bubble I grew up in. He'd recount details from all his exciting foreign travels while serving our community in Congress. I survived adolescence because of the various bits of wisdom he imparted to me from his experience of walking with one foot in each world.

Being the humble dude he is, my dad slept on the pull-out bed of the sofa he sat on while meeting with diplomats in his office on Capitol Hill. He did that to maximize his income for mine and my siblings' upbringing. Congress took him from us on weekdays, but at the end of each week, he'd fly the five and a half hours home. Then he'd turn around and fly back to Washington, DC, the next week. Still, in the morning before school, half awake and barely functioning, we'd gather around the landline speakerphone to pray and read scripture together.

My dad said I was his hero because, even though he didn't share my opinions about equal rights for the LGBTQ+ community, he was proud I fought for the underdog and stood up for my beliefs, no matter the cost. He never once asked me to stop leveraging his reputation to push my own cause.

Lara is my oldest sister, seven years older than me—a true elder millennial. She was like a second mom. Growing up, she would tuck me in and sing me to sleep the nights our mom was away at some political event. Lara spent many nights calming me because for every moment our mom was out past the time she said she'd be home, I'd lie in bed and cry until I heard her footsteps on the wood floor. Only then could I fall asleep.

I idolized Lara and always knew I could trust she would be there for me if I needed to cry about a breakup, even when she didn't fully embrace my being queer. One day, we were helping our sister Katie pick out a new lipstick. Since Katie was indecisive, I put on colors I thought would pop. With each color Lara saw on me, she'd insist Katie try it since we have similar complexions. When the lady working at the store coyly reflected how rare it was for her to see a brother assisting with makeup selection, Lara responded, "We were lucky. We got a gay one." My heart leaped, and I knew Lara saw me.

Jake, who is six years older than me, is the family clown and a royal tease. He's also super grounded. If you need help finding the upside to any troubling situation, he's your guy and will spot the silver lining for you. On top of it all, Jake is incredibly nonjudgmental and shows his love through acts of service.

After Thanksgiving dinner in 2008—when I announced I was no longer suppressing my sexuality and would begin living authentically—the others expressed disapproval, but not Jake. He sat thoughtfully for a while. Due to his silence, our dad asked for his thoughts. Instead of responding, Jake looked at me and asked, "Are you happy, Matt?"

I didn't have to say anything more than, "Yeah, I am."

Jake nodded, smiled, and said, "Okay."

Without another word, he shut down the discussion and affirmed his unconditional love for me. To this day, I aspire to become more like Jake.

Katie sits three years ahead of me and is the most earnest and conscientious of us. She spent our childhood determined to excel at being my sister, persisting even when I rebuffed her efforts to connect. Despite my stony walls, Katie did what she could to chisel her way to my heart. She included me in her activities whenever she could.

When I was in high school, Katie waited up for me each Friday and Saturday night, and we would talk about life during the commercial breaks of our favorite late-night Disney Channel shows. She was always the first to ask me about my dating life and to regularly inquire if I had any romantic interests. Of all of us, she is the most devout in her faith in LDS Church teachings, but she didn't let it keep her from showing up for me.

I love and respect my family dearly. We have grown closer through the years while navigating our conflicting beliefs, and it's awesome to see what stellar parents they have all grown to become.

Since my sexuality became a headline, many insisted I abandon my family, most through anonymous comments online. These outside observers demanded I require my family to reject the foundation upon which they built their lives or turn my back on them forever.

These internet trolls diagnosed me with Stockholm Syndrome and told me it was a shame someone hadn't bullied me into suicide because I forgave the harms caused by my family's previous beliefs and actions. I knew my family would evolve, though, because above all, love matters more.

I was right.

It took me eleven years to accept my own sexuality, given the long-standing indoctrination in which I was born and raised. My family and I were all born and raised in the same environment, except none of them had the inspiration to question our upbringing by an identity that conflicted with it. How could I demand they rapidly reject decades of religious teachings without something internally driving it? It would take time.

I played the long game.

To my great joy, my family didn't need the eleven years I did to accept my sexuality. By leaning into love, we grew stronger than ever.

Not everyone who grows up with disapproving families ends up that lucky. In *this* way, I consider myself fortunate.

Many outside the LGBTQ+ community might not understand the concept of a chosen family, but for those of us who identify lesbian, gay, bisexual, transgender, or otherwise queer, the concept is all too well known. According to a PEW Research study conducted in 2013, approximately four out of ten LGBTQ+ adults surveyed reported being rejected by their families and friends.[2] In my work, specializing in trauma-focused, identity-affirming psychiatric care for LGBTQ+ adolescents and young adults, that number skews higher.

The sad reality is most families act out of fear when rejecting their loved one's identity rather than love. After I started living authentically and dating men, Katie approached me with concern. "I just know gay people are more likely to be depressed, do drugs, and die by suicide," she said. "I don't want that for you."

Like many people, Katie supposed these harms were the result of living—what she considered—the LGBTQ+ *lifestyle*. She assumed statistics explained the lived experience when the truth is that only lived experience can explain statistics.

Over time, research has enhanced our understanding enough to know being LGBTQ+ does not cause these adverse outcomes. The identity rejection, stigma, and intolerance we experience daily from our families, communities of origin, and society-at-large causes these harms.

Several studies show rejection of an individual's sexuality or gender identity *is* the leading contributor to numerous risks faced by LGBTQ+ individuals. These include substance use, homelessness, being a victim to violence, sexually transmitted infections, depression, anxiety, self-harm, suicide, and other mental health issues.[3]

When I spoke to Reverend Rachel Cornwell, parent of a transgender child and author of *Daring Adventures: Helping Gender-Diverse Kids and Their Families Thrive*, she told me because of these risks, she also feared for her child initially.

At five years old, her son cried while telling her, "When I was a star in the sky, I told God I was a boy, but God made me a girl, and now I just have to live with it."

Reverend Cornwell outlined the numerous questions she found herself asking: *Can he really know this at such a young age? Is it the right thing to encourage him to transition or be agnostic about it and just pretend it wasn't happening? Is he going to get bullied? What's going to happen to his body?*

Most compassionate people, like my family and Reverend Cornwell, want what's best for their loved ones because, well, they love them. However, fear and misinformation make it difficult to know the right thing to do and then do it. Recognizing conflicting information in the public, Reverend Cornwell decided to intently search for the correct information.

Through her search, Reverend Cornwell discovered that research on human development supports children can be aware of their gender identity by five years old.[4,5] She also learned while LGBTQ+ children are more likely to have depression and die by suicide, all it takes is *one* accepting and affirming parent in their life to cut that risk nearly in half.[6]

With that, Reverend Cornwell knew she had to trust her son and "follow his lead. The decision was easy at that point," she told me.

Of course, not every gender-divergent person recognizes this early. Most will identify feeling out of place and experience significant discomfort with themselves and their bodies, but not understand why.

Later conceptualization of gender noncongruence can be any of a number of factors, including: more rigid gender norming in their homes, harsh parental reactions to gender nonconforming behaviors (like a boy wanting to play with dolls or wear mom's makeup), or a lack of awareness of the existence of gender diversity.[7] Each of these factors can contribute to adverse mental health outcomes like poor self-worth, anxiety, depression, thoughts of suicide, and even suicide attempts.[8]

For many LGBTQ+ individuals, their families engage in behaviors that end up causing them harm in an attempt to prevent the dangers they fear come from being LGBTQ+. While my family feared for my health and well-being, they mostly feared for my *literal*, eternal salvation. They believed if they didn't guide me away from living "the gay lifestyle," I'd be lost forever.

In Reverend Cornwell's case, she initially feared the bullying and inevitable discrimination her son would face being transgender. She considered whether she could ignore his exploration of his gender identity, hoping it would resolve itself and save him from potential suffering.

In these matters, it's not the thought that counts, unfortunately. The motivation behind such a choice is inconsequential. This type of behavior *will* harm the LGBTQ+ child, regardless.

To understand this phenomenon further, Dr. Caitlin Ryan founded The Family Acceptance Project. She and her team uncovered more than one hundred behaviors families of LGBTQ+ individuals engage in, which are either accepting or rejecting of the individual's identity. They learned rejection includes behaviors and attitudes that try "to change, prevent, deny or minimize their child's LGBTQ+ identity," and can be simple like refusing to talk about it, "not letting their child learn about their LGBTQ+ identity, or excluding them from family events and activities because of their identity."[9]

In my own work, far too often, I encounter parents who expect their children to conform to their expectations rather than adjust to the needs of their children. This stance contributes to great conflict and far more strain on their relationships than is necessary.

You wouldn't treat an orchid like a dandelion and expect it to thrive. That would be ridiculous. An orchid needs specialized care and attention. Meanwhile, dandelions grow in most conditions. If you cared about its survival, you'd learn the best way to nurture the sensitive orchid.

Dr. Brené Brown, a renowned author and researcher of shame and vulnerability, has the guide families need. She leads several courses on parenting and developed "The Wholehearted Parenting Manifesto."

She calls the manifesto her prayer for "when I'm wrestling with vulnerability or when I've got that *never enough* fear." It's her guide for leading her children to become wonderful humans.[10] It begins with "Above all else, I want you to know that you are loved and lovable. You will learn this from my words and actions—the lessons on love are in how I treat you and how I treat myself. I want you to engage with the world from a place of worthiness."[11]

The Family Acceptance Project also developed great resources to help families prevent the harms they fear through support and affirmation. "This includes behaviors like standing up for their child when others mistreat them because of their LGBTQ+ identity and requiring that other family members treat their child with respect—even when they believe being gay or transgender is wrong."[12]

Brown's manifesto is a wonderful framework for doing that. "We will practice courage in our family by showing up, letting ourselves be seen, and honoring vulnerability," it says. "We will always have permission to be ourselves with each other. No matter what, you will always belong here… I will not teach or love or show you anything perfectly, but I will let you see me, and I will always hold sacred the gift of seeing you. Truly deeply seeing you."[13]

Raising a human is no easy task. It's normal if it feels scary, especially when children identify in a way that is foreign and condemned by many who call it immoral. According to

Brown, practicing learning and growing together and giving ourselves permission to live authentically is key.

Mistakes will happen—they are inevitable. However, when we decide love matters more and actively respect each other, repair occurs quickly, and we can avoid long-term consequences.

In my family, the acknowledgments might not have occurred right away, but they did occur. My upbringing instilled in me wonderful values of love, respect, personal responsibility, growth, and standing up for what is right. These values didn't vanish when I chose authenticity like many suppose they do. Leaning into these values got me through the loneliest and most painful parts of my life. My family and I might be in a much different place without them, but we forged our way because we leaned into our love, not away from it.

After all, family is where we first learn how to love and be loved.

CHAPTER 2
The Garden

Someone close to me once said, "Matt, I get why you left the church. If they told me loving my husband was wrong or I couldn't be with him, I would leave too."

While I appreciate her sympathy, I didn't leave the Church of Jesus Christ of Latter-day Saints (LDS or Mormon) because they opposed who I love. If there is a God, I believe they're an unconditionally loving God, without hypocrisy.

That's not the God I learned about in church. The Apostle Matthew advised to judge institutions "by their fruits."[1] I did, and some of the fruits I saw were depression, self-loathing, and suicidal ideation.

That's why I left.

I learned to love others, care for others, and defend the vulnerable at home and in church. That's why I devote my career to caring for the most vulnerable populations. I also learned to trust my inner knowing, and with that came the understanding that religion wasn't God's will at all.

"Oppress not the widow, nor the fatherless, the stranger, nor the poor; and let none of you imagine evil against his brother in your heart," God decreed through Zechariah.[2]

In Matthew, it reads, "Inasmuch as ye have done it unto one of the least of these my brethren, ye have done it unto [Jesus Christ]."[3]

"Love one another"—*this* is God's will.[4]

My dad demonstrated these lessons one day while he and I walked down the street together shopping. A man stopped us and asked for money, which my dad quickly provided. When we walked away, I brutishly asked, "Dad, aren't you worried he's just going to buy alcohol or drugs?"

"Matt, God will judge that man for how he spends the money. He will judge me for whether I gave it to him or not," he replied.

Through this experience, I came to believe Luke's words, "For unto whomsoever much is given, of him shall be much required," meant those who are given much need to recognize how blessed they are—otherwise known as *privileged*.[5] Those given much must look through eyes of compassion rather than judgment. Don't most, if not all, religions preach love and nonjudgment as their foundation?

Despite teachings like these, long-standing traditions within Christian institutions inspire judgment of and harmful attitudes toward others in the hearts of their followers. If you disagree, how do you feel about affirming LGBTQ+

people in their identities and recognizing they are as valid and worthy as you? If your answer is anything but supportive, why do you think that is?

I was nine years old when I recognized others were referring to me when they said, "homosexuality is an abomination." When they compared me to a pedophile because I wanted to experience love and have someone be excited about it with me, I was still a child. I desperately strived for goodness and wielded all my power to achieve it, but at the same time, I learned marrying someone I love would amount to "the sin second to murder."

When I was fourteen years old, after I could no longer bare the shame on my own, I confessed my same-gender attraction to my mom. She then sought counsel from our bishop (a neighborhood church leader), and he referred us to LDS Family Services.

With a desire to provide me with privacy and confidentiality, my mom didn't pry about my visits with the therapist. The therapist, rather than help me process what my mom supposed was healthy curiosity, told me I was addicted to porn and masturbation and treated me for that. When the therapy ended, I told my mom the problem was resolved. She believed I referred to my sexuality, but I was telling her porn and masturbation were no longer a problem.

I think churches are supposed to edify, but that wasn't my experience. I learned to hate myself in church. Although, I don't believe that was the outcome they intended.

Joseph Smith said God told him not to join any of the existing churches because "they draw near to me with their lips, but their hearts are far from me."[6] I wonder if he envisioned his church becoming the same thing.

As with most faiths, LDS Church leaders don't explicitly advocate for animosity toward others. However, it's bound to happen when the foundation of a belief system is on the premise everyone else is incorrect and deceived by Satan if they say otherwise.

It's the same with sexual and gender minorities. Christian religions, like Mormonism, don't teach hatred for LGBTQ+ people, but they use the same damning language, which naturally inspires fear and disdain.

"Hate the sin, love the sinner" was such a common motto. I never understood why they mentioned hate at all. Why not only "love the sinner?"

"Let's love these abominations even though they're deviants who are trying to groom our children" was all I heard.

Thankfully, someone close to me stressed the importance of trusting my connection to God, and He would reveal things to me through my inner knowing. "Matt, I want you to know church leaders and others are going to get it wrong, *even* the prophet," he confided. "It doesn't matter if someone is called of God—and I do believe some are—neither prophets nor churches are God. They are subject to human limitation and bias."

LDS teaching claims everyone is entitled to personal revelation from God regarding His will for their personal life. Still, it can be hard for Mormons to accept personal revelation doesn't always match what their prophets profess.

That's why I was shocked when my friend Wendy Williams Montgomery shared about the time she met Elder Tom Christofferson, one of the LDS Church leaders.

Wendy was one of the first Mama Dragons, an organization of mothers affiliated with religion who support each other in being fierce advocates for their LGBTQ+ children. Wendy wasn't always an advocate for LGBTQ+ rights, however. Before she discovered her thirteen-year-old son Jordan was gay, she participated in the campaign for Prop 8 to ban same-sex marriage in California. When Jordan came out, she found herself confronting the conflict between the values her religion taught and her religion itself.

"One of the main things I got from Mormonism was 'families are forever,'" she told me. "Of course, I should be advocating for his safety, happiness, and mental health."

As her son's peers and community turned their backs—quite literally, they would turn their backs to him at church—she felt hopeless and disillusioned. She said, "It was actually quite surprising when church leaders, my dad, and a couple of my brothers told us *any* version of accepting him was wrong."

Wendy even had to close her business after her church community boycotted and bankrupted her because she became a vocal advocate for her son.

Despite the challenges she faced through her advocacy, they would not silence Wendy and her family. This earned them the attention of Elder Christofferson, who invited Wendy and her husband to meet. In the meeting, Wendy expressed her deep sadness and confusion over being cast out by her faith community for celebrating and defending her son.

Wendy was comforted when he told her, "When we write articles or speak publicly, it's for the majority. We know it's not for everybody. Listen to me when I tell you this: When you receive personal revelation from God, and you recognize it as such, it will *always* trump what we say."

I had goosebumps.

Even with my dad's encouragement to trust my inner knowing, being dismissed as "deceived by Satan" numerous times because I didn't fit the cookie-cutter mold caused me doubt. I felt lost and alone. I threw myself into school and church to escape and hide.

Still, it brought me a sense of peace and challenged me to trust my intuition. It was a skill I found helpful when I first doubted the validity of what I learned, a seed of doubt planted by one of the most wonderful people I knew in high school.

Kim was not LDS but was the most compassionate, Christlike person I had ever met. I hate to say it, but that confused me. It was then, at seventeen years old, that I first realized virtuous people existed outside of the LDS Church,

God's Garden on Earth. Prior to it, I honestly believed someone in tune with God would readily accept it was the *one and only* true church.

As a devout Mormon kid who wanted others to experience the soul-saving "good news" of the LDS Gospel, I did what they trained me to do. I gave Kim a Book of Mormon with thoughtfully highlighted passages, sure to open her heart and mind to the truth.

It couldn't have been more perfect. I mean, she even asked God to guide her to the correct path, and God spoke my name into her heart. Like Joseph Smith alleged, God gave him the truth when he followed the words of James, "If any of you lack wisdom, let him ask of God, that giveth to all men liberally, and upbraideth not; and it shall be given him," I knew Kim would be too.[7]

Kim read, pondered, prayed, and received an answer. I was excited because I knew what her answer would be.

Kim thoughtfully explained that God revealed to her the LDS Church was not for her, and she was doing what she was supposed to.

Obviously, she misunderstood God, right? I trusted it was *the* true church.

I now see, through the eyes of experience, it was Kim who saved me. She opened my mind to the idea there isn't one identical path every person, who has lived and will live, must follow to find happiness and eternal life.

It's unfortunate this isn't the norm. Come on. Billions of people have lived in the world, and you mean to tell me only one circumscribed way of living allows you peace in the afterlife?

I get it, though.

Back then, for me to accept Mormonism wasn't the only path for every single person would mean the foundation upon which I built my belief system was false and, therefore, could all be false.

Those I asked to help me understand my confusion dismissed it, saying Kim was "deceived by Satan." She was more Christlike than any of them. I couldn't dismiss her experience because it didn't mirror my own.

When we have certain blessings, regardless of what they are, it can be difficult to understand the perspective of someone who doesn't share them. Often, we expect others to want what we have and believe they'd want us to share it with them. This mindset can be assumptive and isolates those who have different values and ideas about what adds meaning to life.

It's human and possible to evolve from. To evolve is a choice.

Many who think they behave *morally* cause inadvertent harm to others because they forget the greatest law is love. Like me, Jordan was also sure he'd go to hell due to the damning messages he'd internalized from all the *good Christians* who forgot to love.

"When you and Dad and all of my brothers and sisters are in heaven, where am I going to be?" he asked Wendy, struggling to speak between sobs.

That was a turning point for Wendy. "It just broke me. I'm like, *What have I taught this sweet boy?*" she told me with tears in her eyes. "Jordan, heaven is wherever you are. We will all be together wherever that is. It's not going to be heaven without you," she replied.

Both Wendy and I still hold many of the values we gained from our LDS upbringing, even after moving away from religious practice. This experience is common. It's contrary to the narratives I encountered in my youth regarding LGBTQ+ individuals who were "deceived by Satan" and "abandoned their morality" when they chose to live openly and authentically.

These stories about prodigal children who left God's Garden haunted me in my youth. With the stories came the assurance, "You can leave, but you'll come back—they all do," which triggered hopelessness in me because I was suffering there.

Like many prodigal children who left the Garden before me, I took the journey and became a better person because of it. I realized I could only live the values I gained in religion if I left religion and trusted my inner knowing. I would no longer allow worldly institutions, like churches, to dictate how or who I love.

Too often, people struggle to escape the hopelessness phase, like I did. A study published in the *Journal of Adolescence* explored the impact of growing up Christian on LGBTQ+ youth in the United States. Feelings of worthlessness, depression, and strain in family and peer relationships were common among the participants; 80 percent of whom were raised LDS, and the rest were either Catholic or Presbyterian.[8]

Luckily, growing up religious can have some positive impacts. LGBTQ+ individuals raised religious tended to have a stronger sense of self and acceptance of others' experiences. They found, "Religiosity may serve a protective benefit for some sexual minorities who integrate childhood religious values into their overall identity."[9]

The researchers also concluded growing up in these contexts contributed to greater resilience and ability to overcome adversity. That "is highlighted in their ability to espouse a more open-minded worldview and carefully select the values from their religious upbringing which complement their identity."[10] The trouble is they develop the ability to overcome adversity because they experience Christianity as adversity.

I can attest to the study's results from my own experience. One of the greatest lessons the church ever taught me is adversity is meant for growth. Throughout my religious instruction, I frequently heard the scripture, "God is faithful, who will not suffer you to be tempted above that ye are able; but will with the temptation also make a way to escape, that ye may be able to bear it."[11]

I treated pain like a trial I could learn from and use to grow into my divinity by recognizing the strengths I gained along my journey.

I suppose it's not ironic my greatest adversity was religion—a garden of trauma that gave me tools to overcome it. Adversarial growth like this, or the effect coping with trial has on improving resilience, supports Nietzsche's old saying, "What doesn't kill you, [may] make you stronger."[12]

It's important to note this does not suggest adversity alone is beneficial. The research supports adopting a mindset that considers adversity an opportunity for growth inspires resilience. It's incredibly protective but is not a replacement for a safe and affirming support system.[13]

If it weren't for the supportive scaffolding and system of values my family raised me with, I likely wouldn't have navigated the identity rejection and suppression during my youth as I did. I'm not saying it didn't traumatize me immensely. I am saying that foundation provided me with a much speedier, holistic recovery from it.

What are the fruits of your faith?

CHAPTER 3
Pursuit of Happiness

"It's time America realized that there was no gay exemption in the right to 'life, liberty, and the pursuit of happiness' in the Declaration of Independence," urged Barry Goldwater, former US Senator from Arizona and Republican nominee for president of the United States of America.[1] He was one of the first Republicans who challenged politicians and voters to change their stance on equal rights for LGBTQ+ Americans.

"I am a conservative Republican, but I believe in democracy and the separation of church and state. The foundation of the conservative movement is on the simple tenet that people have the right to live life as they please, as long as they don't hurt anyone else in the process. No one has ever shown me how being gay or lesbian harms anyone else," Goldwater continued. "Even the 1992 Republican platform affirms the principle that 'bigotry has no place in our society.' ...The party faithful must not let it happen. Anybody who cares about real moral values understands that this isn't about granting *special* rights—it's about protecting *basic* rights."[2]

His words were published in 1994, and thirty years later, we continue to debate whether a significant portion of citizens are equal under the law. Even the most recent Republican platform from 2016, readopted in 2020, affirms a commitment to ending discrimination and prejudice.

It says, "We denounce bigotry, racism, anti-Semitism, ethnic prejudice, and religious intolerance… Our ranks include Americans from every faith and tradition, and we respect the right of each American to follow his or her deeply held beliefs."[3]

In practice, that seems to only be true if you espouse the same beliefs they do.

My favorite part of the Declaration of Independence has always been, "All men are created equal, that they are endowed by their Creator with certain unalienable Rights, that among these are Life, Liberty, and the pursuit of Happiness."[4] I even have the words, "Life," "Liberty," and "Happiness" tattooed in a crest on my back, behind my heart. It symbolizes the creed protecting my right to love who I choose.

I realize most kids probably didn't grow up with a favorite part of the Declaration of Independence, but when your dad is a US Congressman and your mom is a political activist, life isn't typical. When I turned eighteen years old, my mom's first gift to me was a voter registration form.

We attended all sorts of events, surrounded by some of the most powerful people in the world, including members of Congress, diplomats, and presidents. It felt important to be part of such a powerful group of people. I often felt like an outsider, but I thought being a congressman's son made me more interesting.

The biggest trouble I faced being a congressman's son was feeling I could never properly be a kid. My mom set high standards for how to behave, reminding us we each carried the potential to harm my dad's reputation. She instilled the fear of God and the liberal media within me. If I were to do something that got me into trouble, it would be first-page news: "When Mormon, Republican Congressman's Son Behaves Badly."

I remember vividly from my father's campaigns that he was good at connecting with the people he served, like I am sure most politicians hope to be. He often told personal stories to prove he meant what he said, or he would fight for what he promised.

When my sister Lara became a teacher, he would tie her into his views on education, saying something like, "My daughter is a teacher. When I say I'll bring money back to the classroom, you can count on that." You could count on it too. He often inquired about our passions to learn how to make better informed policy decisions for related issues.

I think voters enjoy knowing you have some sort of stake in whatever you promise. People trust fathers and mothers will do what they can to fight for their children to have successful and happy lives. Voters expect their representatives to "promote the general Welfare and secure the Blessings of Liberty to ourselves and our Posterity," because the Founding Fathers intended it.[5]

I believed my dad made examples of us to prove he would fight for us, even if it wasn't always what a majority of his voters wanted.

After I began living authentically queer, I realized that wasn't the case—not for me, anyway. What I would have given to hear, "My son is gay. When I say I'll bring equality to all people, you can count on that."

Unfortunately for the LGBTQ+ community, his voters didn't want a representative who would fight for *those people's* life, liberty, and happiness. Voters care if you have a stake in the game when it aligns with their beliefs, but if not, they demand loyalty, even if it means harming your own child. That's what the people of my father's district asked for; a man who would prove his loyalty to them by promising to oppose the liberty of his son.

Like his constituents, I could have demanded my dad be loyal to me or lose me forever, but that's not my style. Instead, I chose faith and patience over hostility. I opted to love my dad despite his views, hoping one day his heart would change.

While I waited for that day, I engaged him in many discussions about his views to find points of common ground. I also established boundaries and expectations for my psychological safety. For several years, that meant maintaining emotional distance from my family. It required playing the long game from afar.

Eventually, my patience won, and his views evolved after he left office. Today, he believes, "People should be able to make most of their decisions free from government interference, including things coming from the Republican Party that are anti-LGBTQ+," he said while I discussed this book with him. "I think if a school teaches something you don't want, move to another school, but you shouldn't come up with a law that says, 'You can't teach this.'"

Since his tenure in Congress, he has spoken out about the harms of SOGIECE and advocated at the Arizona State Legislature for its ban. When he ran for governor of Arizona in 2022, he promised me that if elected, he would do all he could for the advancement of LGBTQ+ rights, even if it meant writing an executive order.

The Founding Fathers didn't intend the Constitution of the United States to remain forever unchanged. "Whenever any Form of Government becomes destructive of these ends, it is the Right of the People to alter or to abolish it," they instructed.[6]

Humans are, and always have been, incredibly diverse. One individual's "pursuit of Happiness" might look different from another's, but each should be granted the liberty—freedom from oppressive restrictions—to pursue happiness and experience the fullness of life.

I believe these words confirm the Founding Fathers understood that even though time changes and people evolve, a person's access to these three rights should always be secured. When the government infringes upon these rights, the people *should* change it.

I have this fairy tale notion our representatives go to bat for us to protect our individual freedoms. At each new term, members of Congress take an oath to "support and defend the Constitution of the United States,"[7] including a promise to "promote the general Welfare and secure the Blessings of Liberty to ourselves and our Posterity."[8]

In my opinion, that oath extends the right to "Life, Liberty and the pursuit of Happiness" to *all* people, not only their voters.

Somewhere along the way, many representatives decide they can prescribe millions of people a single version of what they think constitutes "Happiness," and demand we accept that. We expect them to make better decisions than we could.

Instead, they restrict our liberty and tell us what life should look like for us rather than representing with the *consent of the governed*. Starting in 2011, a majority of *the governed* supported same-gender marriage, which reached 71 percent approval in May 2023, according to Gallup.[10] Rather than affirm all identities are valid, we have to keep revisiting this process over and over like some newly visible identity will ever be less deserving.

Is love not included in "the pursuit of Happiness?"

It seems many people truly don't believe love is part of happiness. It's like they refuse to accept love can exist between anyone other than one man and one woman. If marriage "is the foundation for a free society," why block millions of people from accessing it?[10]

I met with Neil Giuliano, former mayor of Tempe, Arizona, to understand his perspective—that of a gay man who was Republican during his tenure in politics. "Individual

They said I was perverse and needed therapy to convert to heterosexuality, but somehow, LGBTQ+ people are the ones grooming children. Go figure.

Don't get me started on that. Conservative and religious communities are harming LGBTQ+ young people through conversion but will find a way to martyr themselves. That's psychological abuse, friends.

I know this firsthand from my own experience with LGBTQ+ conversion in my youth. The abuse I suffered from the experience led to years of worthlessness, self-loathing, and doubt.

When my grandpa passed away, I connected how important it was to follow my own path and pursue happiness like I experienced it, not dictated by others. After graduating from Arizona State University, I decided to live with my dad's parents because they had each been in and out of the hospital, and I wanted to help.

I only lived there for three months when my grandpa passed away.

I awoke in the morning to my grandma frantically crying for me to help her. I raced into my grandpa's room and found him on the ground, without a pulse or observable breath. I told my grandma to call 911, and I began CPR.

In my heart, I knew it was too late, but I wanted to give her a few more moments of hope that her love of more than fifty years could be saved. I gave compressions, liberty—conservatism at its core—should be to stay out of people's lives. Religions can have whatever laws, rules, or sacraments they want. That's not the government," Neil opined. "Many believe they need to insert themselves into other people's lives like they're society's Savior. They believe they're called to oppose people who just want to live full lives and pursue happiness. I'm talking about them activating their deeply held religious beliefs on the rest of society that doesn't share their beliefs. It's really terrible."

It's also counterproductive to the maintenance of a stable foundation for society. "Our relationships are the same," Neil continued. "Give us the same respect you give any other relationship. It's not about sex. It's about respecting relationships. It's not hard."

The natural orientation of humans is to love. What's gender got to do with it? Why do some believe LGBTQ+ people are only capable of lust and only straight people can love?

Those who think this way are the first to say queer people are perverse. These are the same people who, when they hear "gay," the thought that comes to mind is *gay sex*.

Stop thinking about that.

If you ask me, that's why, across the country, politicians are trying to pass laws to keep us from saying "gay." The word gives them *sexy* thoughts.

When I hear the word "gay," I think of individuals who love each other, often in the face of danger and chronic discrimination.

disturbed by the sound of his ribs cracking under my hands, completely unprepared for how violent cardio-pulmonary resuscitation was.

When the paramedics arrived, they quickly declared him dead. I called each of his children to inform them what happened while the neighbors took care of my grandma. Their spouses answered my calls, and I can still feel the despair that echoed in their voices through broken sobs as I shared the news with them, one by one.

My grandpa's death also showed me the importance of being honest with those I love. I regret I never told him I was queer out of respect for his children. When I volunteered to move in with him, they required I hide my truth, assuring me it would be the death of him.

I accepted that was truth.

Except, he died anyway. What really pains me is my grandpa was incredibly loving and nonjudgmental. He loved fully and was the only person I didn't doubt loved me unconditionally. At least twice daily while living with him, I'd catch him looking at me. When I'd turn to him, he would say, "I sure do love you, Matt," and I knew it was true.

A few months after his death, I had a dream. I found myself in a dark, empty room on my hands and knees, with my head bowed down. When someone approached me, I looked up, and my eyes locked with my grandpa's. He was beaming with joy. I jumped up, raced to him, and threw my arms around him.

With tears running down my face, I asked, "Grandpa, what is it all about? What's the point?"

"To live and be happy," he replied.

"Is it okay I am gay?" I asked.

Without hesitation and a look of wonder on his face, he said, "Of course it is," and he hugged me tighter.

In an instant, he was gone, and I awoke. It may have been a dream, but because of it, I gave myself permission to trust, like everyone else, I deserved the right to my brand of happiness. Through that dream, I could channel the unending love my grandfather had provided me while he was alive. A love, prior to that experience, I hadn't been able to offer myself.

I've concluded many of our leaders are simply lost. Like my aunts and uncles were, they are afraid if we let love be love, it will be the death of something they hold dear. Conservatives are convinced they are defending tradition and traditional values, fearing if they allow all the right to pursue happiness, it will damage the basic fabric of our society.

It's wild they don't see that through their defense of tradition, they act against the most basic principles established by the Founding Fathers when they wrote the Declaration of Independence and Constitution of the United States of America. These traditions were meant for *all* citizens.

When the Founding Fathers established these practices, which they suggested should change when not serving the public, it was a different time. Humans enslaved other humans. Thankfully, we recognized the need to evolve and invited those our forefathers enslaved to enjoy the same traditions previously only granted White people. People once believed expanding the definition of tradition to include interracial marriage would harm society and only legalized these unions in 1965.[11]

Neither evolution destroyed society.

The evolution of tradition does not signify its downfall. Considering LGBTQ+ people equal and deserving of the life they choose, the liberty to live it, and happiness how they experience it does not damage the "foundation of a free society."[12]

We have a problem, especially here in the United States of America. Some think it's acceptable to limit another individual's freedom for no other reason than they disagree with how the other lives their life. This is neither the foundation of a healthy nor a free society.

It may be tradition, but it doesn't have to be. We have to stop constraining others' capacity to live their lives how they desire when it harms no one.

Perhaps the greater threat to a free society is the weaponization of puritanical morality against others by legal mandate.

PART II
DIVISION

CHAPTER 4

Monopoly

"Of all the forms of inequality, injustice in health is the most shocking and the most inhuman because it often results in physical death," the Reverend Dr. Martin Luther King, Jr. said while at the second convention of the Medical Committee for Human Rights in 1966.[1] His words continue to ring true today. We also have a clear understanding inequality and injustice contribute to poor health outcomes, including chronic disability and premature death.

According to the World Health Organization (WHO), "Depending on the nature of [their] environments, different groups will have different experiences of material conditions, psychosocial support, and behavioural options, which make them more or less vulnerable to poor health. Social stratification likewise determines differential access to and utilization of health care, with consequences for the inequitable promotion of health and well-being, disease prevention, and illness recovery and survival."[2]

This understanding amplifies the significance of King's words and supports the need for dramatic change in the structure of our society. Changing healthcare delivery is not enough to address the disparities of minorities.

Many doctors have encountered this challenge—trying whatever options we can to improve people's conditions. Colloquially, this phenomenon is often called "Shit Life Syndrome," a term reserved for those whose physical and mental health problems are the result of their social status.[3]

I am grateful for the opportunity to become a child, adolescent, and adult psychiatrist to help heal the kinds of injustices I experienced in my youth, something I likely wouldn't have done if it weren't for the pain I went through.

After earning my bachelor's in psychology, I completed medical school, a residency to specialize in general psychiatry, and a fellowship to subspecialize in child and adolescent psychiatry. It was a total of thirteen years of education and training after high school.

After finishing my fellowship at MedStar Georgetown University Hospital, I accepted a position at Whitman Walker Health System, a community-based center in Washington, DC. I am currently the manager of psychiatry. My work primarily focuses on the mental health needs of the LGBTQ+, racialized, and economically disadvantaged people living in DC, Maryland, and Virginia.

Through my work, I quickly realized medical and mental health treatments were totally inadequate to meet the needs of the people I serve. The troubles I felt called to confront wouldn't resolve while social and structural disparities persist—like bias on account of race, gender, sexual orientation, and ability. It often seems like I'm just spraying air freshener in a stable, hoping the manure won't stink.

These injustices, often called "tradition," led me to seek out more tools I could utilize. For that reason, I completed a master's in health and public interest, a multidisciplinary degree that includes courses in public health, policy, and advocacy, at Georgetown University. While there, I decided to write this book to give what I've learned along the way to the public.

I'm not here to demonize anyone. We *all* have prejudices that impact our day-to-day behaviors, including how we treat others. It's normal to develop an us versus them mentality. It's human to resist what we perceive as different. It's also easy to suppose our beliefs and opinions don't affect others.

I'm here to tell you they do.

We all carry unintended biases, but we are not all bigoted. The two are not the same. I know this is a charged issue, which makes many defensive and closed off to considering how implicit biases impact their behaviors.

A history of overt racism programmed us, and it didn't go away with the freeing of slaves or when segregation ended. That history impacted policies and beliefs in ways we haven't resolved. It contributed to stereotypes and opinions that aren't valid. It's not our fault society brought us up with them, but it is our responsibility to recognize and correct them when we learn about them.

These systemic biases are handed down from generations before, woven into the structure of society, and can be difficult to recognize and resolve. When left unchecked, they inspire beliefs and practices that become the *norm*, even if they aren't correct. People then adopt them, and the cycle of harm to those with less power perpetuates through the democratic process.

Consider the game Monopoly. Imagine you are playing, and the game is set up such that everyone else starts with more money than you and can move double the spaces with each turn.

Certainly, you might protest, but what if you didn't have a choice over whether you played the game or not? What if that was the life into which you were born? What if the other players insisted the game was completely fair and you simply needed to become more *self-reliant*?

Since the inheritance of wealth is generational, the effects of slavery and segregation still create huge wealth gaps today—even if we assume discrimination completely stopped with the end of segregation. It didn't, by the way. If your grandfather was denied a job because he was Black, he wouldn't be able to afford to send his kids to college. That would limit their opportunities to get high-paying jobs, and the cycle continues.

Just like in the game, it's not that you aren't capable compared to the other players. Our initial conditions produce an inherent disadvantage for some. It isn't any one person's fault or the result of any conscious decision. Rather, it's the unintended consequence of our history and the way governments and societies establish themselves. This is what is meant by *systemic bias*—when certain groups are inherently disadvantaged and others favored.

What if when you passed Go, you could not collect $200, but others did? Or you had to put more money down to purchase a property? Or when people landed on your property, they didn't have to pay you, but you'd have to pay them if you landed on theirs?

Systemic bias in society adds extra layers of difficulty for some individuals to access opportunities and resources, simply because of traits they were born with. These opportunities and resources can include education, healthcare, fairness in criminal justice, safe housing, healthy food, and clean water.

In wealthier districts, schools have access to more resources and opportunities, while schools in other districts have less. No one intended that to be the case. These children are set up to either work much harder to rise above their lot in life or persist from a disadvantaged position throughout their lives and careers.

These challenges, which are not the fault of the individual, contribute to stereotypes about them and the groups they belong to. People then adopt these stereotypes as proof of their biased beliefs, further contributing to the problem.

It does not mean we can't carry the beliefs we have. What it does mean is we must be diligent about how we behave because of them, to keep them from impacting others. The law protects our right to our beliefs, but the law does not grant us the right to impose them on other people. We see this with efforts to block others' access to healthcare that would significantly help them, like gender-affirming medical treatments or identity-affirming psychotherapies.

This is the trouble with systemic bias. It ultimately affects how we think about another's experience, which contributes to how we treat them.

Consider the experience of Leandra Stanley, who identifies as Black and is the director of diversity and inclusion at Comscore, Inc. When I met with Leandra, she told me about growing up with a dream of going into musical theater. At fourteen years old, Leandra, who was six feet tall and larger than life, tried out for the school musical. Because of her beautiful singing voice, they asked her to sing the lead—only sing.

They asked Leandra to hide backstage and sing while a petite, White girl was in the spotlight, lip-syncing. While talented, they deemed Leandra "ineligible to be the romantic lead of a hokey country play," she told me. "That really changed the trajectory of how I viewed myself and many things going forward."

Leandra encountered many spaces where, because she showed up authentically, people treated her like "I was going to have a negative impact on the people around me. I really didn't experience what it was like to feel right, like I belong, or like I'm not this deviant that's going to poison the water around me, until I was in my midtwenties."

Politicians say it is up to individuals to pull themselves out of their troubling circumstances. They assert it's neither the responsibility of society nor the government to assist—the ol' "Pull yourself up by your bootstraps" routine, a feat which is literally impossible. How is that the ideal?

The problem here is the structure of society and the systems in place actively cause these troubles, while falsely promising equal access to opportunity. The same people would probably point to examples of individuals who started out in challenging situations and overcame them, achieving a life of means.

First, that is not the norm. Second, if that were all it took, why do Black women with financial means and a college education die in childbirth at significantly higher rates than White women with the same characteristics? Why is it they also die at higher rates than White women who didn't finish high school or are low-income?[4] Clearly, taking *personal responsibility* to achieve a life of means and higher education isn't enough.

What is?

Several categories of people start from a place of disadvantage, be it related to power, wealth, or ability. Addressing systemic bias isn't about giving them special treatment. It's about ensuring everyone has a fair shot at success by starting from a secure place that aligns with the core American values of fairness and equality.

It's about acknowledging these unseen hurdles and working toward systems that genuinely offer equal opportunities to everyone, regardless of their background. Many people spend a great portion of their lives, if not their whole lives, without basic needs for survival, including physiological, safety, love and belonging, esteem, and self-actualization.

According to Abraham Maslow, when these needs go unmet, an individual can persist in survival mode, or an excessively stressed state, and struggle to thrive or achieve.[5] His theory seems to hold true across cultures according to more recent studies looking at need fulfillment and subjective well-being. Need fulfillment is not only achieved by the individual but is also highly correlated with the society in which we live, especially basic physiological and safety needs.[6]

When we consider those impacted by systemic biases—people who generally lack at least one, if not more, of these basic needs—it's understandable they exist in a perpetually stressed state. When faced with disparities like wealth and health inequality or difficulty accessing resources and opportunities, people cannot focus on growth and progress.

I spoke with Dr. Eric Wright, a professor of sociology and public health at Emory University. He explained another leading factor is the social disconnect resulting from social disparities and stereotypes.

"When people don't have social connections that are accepting, and you see this with minority groups, especially Black and LGBTQ+, they have higher suicide rates," Wright informed me. "We see that same thing among people with serious mental illnesses or any group that experiences challenges finding social acceptance and community.

Typically, they have worse mental health outcomes across the board."

According to medical sociologists, Drs. Martha Lang and Chloe Bird, "Societal problems such as segregation, poverty, racism, homophobia, and transphobia can cause emotional and physical stress to the body, and these stressors have been demonstrated to have a direct negative impact on health."[7]

I had the privilege of taking a course in medical sociology from Dr. Lang at Georgetown University, during the summer of 2022. When I asked about her research related to LGBTQ+ young people, she said, "Imagine what the impact is for young people, queer people growing up, with war declared, especially on trans folks. For young people, that developmental phase of identity is profound. To have that identity challenged is having a profound effect on them."

Living with chronically elevated stress has a powerfully negative impact on health, likely tied to the effects of prolonged exposure to stress hormones, according to the WHO.[8] Temporary, self-limited elevations of stress hormones are typical and important for survival and achievement. However, the human body is not meant to experience high levels of these hormones for prolonged periods of time, like we see with population groups that are disadvantaged due to social inequity.

These prolonged, high levels of stress contribute to the dysregulation of multiple major body systems, including metabolic (cholesterol, weight, blood sugar, etc.), immunologic (healing, inflammation, etc.), cardiovascular (stroke, blood pressure, etc.), and neuroendocrine (testosterone, estrogen, cortisol, etc.).

Like Dr. Martin Luther King almost sixty years ago, and after three years of analyzing decades of research, the WHO's Commission on Social Determinants of Health concluded, "Social justice is a matter of life and death. It affects the way people live, their consequent chance of illness, and their risk of premature death... The conditions in which people live and die are, in turn, shaped by political, social, and economic forces. Social and economic policies have a determining impact on whether a child can grow and develop to its full potential and live a flourishing life, or whether its life will be blighted."[9]

Population health and well-being are not solely the responsibility of the healthcare industry. The onus belongs to all of us and should be shared across sectors, especially in research, agriculture, housing, and education.

In research, it's common to separate people into categories like race, gender, sexuality, and income or education level to identify differences between them. The problem with this is that people usually blame the identified differences on group genetics, which contributes to group stereotyping.

Prior to understanding how much of health is socially determined, I incorrectly assumed higher rates of type 2 diabetes among racialized minorities were a combination of genetic predisposition and poor choices. However, due to social inequality, racialized individuals are gentrified (*cough* segregated) into nutrition-deficient areas and have reduced capacity to access education, healthcare, and decent jobs with benefits. They also suffer the metabolic effects of elevated stress hormones from facing daily prejudice.

I have personally experienced the damaging effects of systemic bias and how it impacted the beliefs and opinions of those around me. Others saw me more for what made me different than what made us the same. People I deeply cared for considered me defective, deviant, and a problem to purge from the world, simply because of the gender of the person I'd someday love and want to share my life with.

My family raised me to love others without judgment. Then I became an *other* and was treated with disdain—judged for an innate characteristic I had no more control over than being right-handed.

My mental health declined. My faith community ostracized me and barred me from going on a Mormon proselytizing mission to serve God. Friends stopped associating with me. Acquaintances and strangers maligned me. I've feared for my safety because of the threats I received. When I became an *other*, I became a statistic.

These are the costs of othering.

The costs are great, and we cannot ignore them. Maybe a time existed when tribalism was necessary for survival, but nowadays, it contributes to social disconnection and loneliness, especially when the options are either to conform or be mandated to.

CHAPTER 5
Neurofabulous

In Mormonism, they consider eight as the *age of accountability*. It is the age at which "Heavenly Father knows we are old enough to be responsible for our actions."[1]

Basically, your eighth birthday is the day you become a sinner.

Happy birthday!
You can go to hell now!
Oh, and much of the excruciating pain Christ felt while blood poured from every pore, before he died, while nailed to a cross, for you to be the selfish sinner you are, will be your fault.
Be grateful.

Ironically, or not, eight was the age I developed obsessive-compulsive disorder (OCD)—the religious type.

"I have a strange feeling always with me I can't figure out. I think I haven't been where I would like on a spiritual standing, like I haven't followed the commandments close enough," I wrote in my journal on February 16, 2003.

"These feelings keep coming, but I believe they come from my thoughts, which aren't always good. I realized, though, that these thoughts don't come to me because I want them. They are in my head because Satan wants them there. It isn't my fault for my thoughts unless I don't fight them right away. Then, it is my fault for keeping them."

Each day, I spent hours obsessing I'd suffer for eternity because intrusive sexual thoughts, fears of violence perpetrated against me, or of acting on harmful impulses plagued my mind. Intense shame and anxiety filled me.

I believed I had to confess everything and pray excessively for forgiveness. When I woke and multiple times throughout the day, I'd pray, seeking forgiveness for any impure thought I had. Then again, at night, I'd beg God to end it all. I truly believed Satan was targeting me, and if I wasn't diligent, he'd win.

Anytime I had physical contact with anyone, my OCD pushed sexual thoughts about them into my mind, even if it was my own family member. At night when I lay in bed, scenarios of home invasion and someone coming to either kill or rape me played out in my mind on repeat. I'd compulsively plan out what I would do should any of it come to pass. If I didn't open my eyes repetitively, I was sure someone would attack me. I had to stay vigilant. It could take hours to fall asleep.

Once I recognized my attraction to men and the reality of what it meant for me, a young Mormon, my OCD became relentless. OCD didn't cause my queerness or make me confused about my sexuality. Such narratives exist but are completely unfounded. It did significantly magnify my shame.

It was one more cross I believed God asked me to bear. The promise, "God is faithful, who will not suffer you to be tempted above that ye are able; but will with the temptation also make a way to escape, that ye may be able to bear it," was my reassurance.[2]

I convinced myself since Satan was targeting me this intensely, God must have big plans for me. I prayed longer, fasted frequently to demonstrate my devotion, studied scripture twice a day, and sought any opportunity to wish God would take it all away.

Before bed, I'd pray and ask God if I could wake up the next day to learn my life was nothing more than a nightmare. Each day, I'd awaken to repeat that nightmare again.

I ultimately came to believe I was perverse because of the thoughts. I didn't understand it was a condition of my mind producing the thoughts or that I didn't have to listen to them.

Since I went undiagnosed until my late twenties, you might wonder if my family is one of those that "don't believe in mental health," like many of my clients describe their own. The truth is, they didn't really understand mental health conditions. Then again, most don't.

If you recall, my mom even took me to see an LDS therapist, but he declared me a porn and masturbation addict instead of exploring my sexuality questions or obsessive fear of eternal damnation.

Because my OCD masqueraded as hyper-religiosity, those around me supposed I was just an intense little zealot. I'm sure if they recognized I was experiencing a mental health issue, they absolutely would have gotten me the help I needed.

It overwhelmed even my mom because I confessed it all to her. She tolerated it for a while, until I confessed the intrusive images I had of sexually gratifying Jesus. "That's enough!" she exclaimed. "I don't want to hear it anymore."

I complied.

These days, the LDS Church acknowledges religious OCD disproportionately affects its members. Church leaders raise awareness about it, according to my sister Katie. Unfortunately, it was not in time for me to benefit.

Like it is for me, the thoughts and compulsions associated with OCD are unwanted and do not align with the sufferer's values. The types of OCD vary greatly and are likely the result of intense dread or a traumatic experience. OCD tends to hyper-fixate on what a person fears most. In my case, my great fear was spending eternity without my family because Satan won my soul.

OCD is more common in people who apply greater meaning to their thoughts and believe their thoughts are facts. People with OCD, like mine, face internal shame and stigmas, and people who do not understand treat them as dangerous. This attitude toward OCD is harmful because it leads those with OCD to conceal what they are experiencing rather than seek help for it.

The truth is, people with disturbing, intrusive thoughts from OCD do not act on them. The compulsions they engage in are typically an effort to prevent the thoughts from becoming reality.

Most everyone experiences intrusive thoughts, to a degree. If you've ever driven down the road and imagined crashing the car, wrapping it around a tree while gas begins to leak, and the engine sets fire, that's an intrusive thought. Most will not think about it long—unless, of course, that's what they want to do.

In OCD, intrusive thoughts become near constant, and those with them fear they'll occur. Dr. Patrick McGrath, chief clinical officer at NOCD, an organization specializing in OCD treatment, explains intrusive thoughts likely stem from our survival instinct. They are the mind's way of alerting us to possibilities for which we need to be on guard should they occur. According to McGrath, OCD lies to us and says, "If it's always at the top of your mind, you'll never be surprised."[3]

You know, prepare for the worst. Logically, the individual knows the occurrence has a low probability, but *what if this time is that slim chance?*

OCD is also more common in people with more black-and-white thinking, like in autism, another characteristic of mine I only learned of when I was about thirty. Autism is also a widely misunderstood and highly stigmatized experience people view like it's something "you wouldn't wish on someone," a phrase I've heard numerous times.

Even "well-trained professionals from most mental health disciplines also subscribe to stereotypes about mental illness," research concludes.[5] I've seen this in my own practice. Many of my clients come to me with stories of past providers dismissing their concerns and belittling their experiences, especially those with other stigmatized identities.

Seventy percent of people worldwide go untreated for mental health conditions due to factors like "(1) lack of knowledge about the features and treatability of mental illnesses, (2) ignorance about how to access assessment and treatment, [and] (3) prejudice against people who have mental illness."[4] On a grand scale, we see this sort of discrimination lead to scapegoating—using stereotypes to misplace blame onto a stigmatized population.

Recently, I attended a conference hosted by Massachusetts General Hospital where the *autism specialist* taught about how to medicate autism, "you know, the classic kind where they don't talk, and they hit themselves." He spoke of medications for treating various challenges commonly associated with autism. However, we use the same medications to treat the same challenges in someone who isn't autistic.

Misinformation about autism is widespread. I believe that's largely due to mental health authorities falsely labeling it a disorder. Rather than seeing it for what it really is, a common variation of human neurodevelopment, it's treated like a problem to overcome—a burden to all involved.

While autistic people are more likely to experience disorder in their lives, that's the case with anyone who doesn't fit the mold society expects we should. Because we don't fit the mold, others tell us we must change and adapt to the ones around us. We are the ones who have greater difficulty adapting, but it becomes our responsibility to conform so those around us can feel *comfortable*.

I have worked with numerous individuals I am certain are autistic, who come to me with psychological evaluations that dismiss the likelihood they are because they "made eye contact and engaged in conversation," like that's all there is to it. These are individuals who, like me, have learned to *mask* or conform to those around them.

When interacting with others, I have to deliberately prompt myself to look at people's faces, but I blur them out because eye contact is uncomfortable. I also have a running dialogue in my head telling me: *You've looked long enough. Look away and then look back. They said something sad, make the sad face. Raise your eyebrows. Laugh halfheartedly.* If I didn't, I'd probably look irritated or perplexed all the time.

Like me, Leandra Stanley, mentioned in chapter 4, is autistic and has ADHD. Leandra had a similar experience to mine and informed me, "Through my entire educational experience, I went undiagnosed and always had trouble learning but was regarded like a natural leader. I had much potential I was told I was not living up to. You know, that typical narrative. I couldn't understand why I felt different." The journey to understanding led Leandra to become a DEI specialist to learn how to harness the strengths autism and ADHD provide.

Neurodiversity is a paradigm that considers all humans have a certain neurotype or way their brain developed to process information. Each type has its own strengths and weaknesses; strengths to channel and weaknesses to strengthen. Each needs the right environmental conditions for success.

Michael Whitehouse, an entrepreneur with ADHD, considers neurodivergence a superpower and shared metaphors with me that are helpful for understanding it. The way he tells it, "Superman on Krypton is just some dude. I think he's a rich dude, but just some dude. You put him under a yellow sun, and he's got superpowers. If he landed on a planet where they built walls out of kryptonite, it would have disabled him. It all depends on where you put him."

Michael suggests we think of neurotypes like the classes of characters in Dungeons and Dragons. "There is a *normal*, but this is a nonclass, and it's not good. Everyone's got a class like fighter, cleric, magic user, and so on. Some of them are more common; some of them are less common. You wouldn't consider the fighters disabled because they can't use magic. You don't call the magic user disabled because they can't use heavy weapons. And you wouldn't have a party only of fighters. It wouldn't make any sense. You want to have a mix of them. It's the same thing on a team."

Many companies understand the importance of having diverse abilities on teams and have started recruiting neurodivergent talent, according to *Harvard Business Review*. Like Michael, they recognize neurodivergent individuals have "higher-than-average abilities; research shows some conditions, including autism and dyslexia, can bestow special skills in pattern recognition, memory, or mathematics."[6]

Neurodivergent people often require accommodations or adjustments to the role or work environment to enhance their capacity to perform. Many companies find providing accommodations pays off significantly through "productivity gains, quality improvement, boosts in innovative capabilities, and broad increases in employee engagement."[7]

These organizations are on the forefront of progress, even before many mental health professionals. They recognize neurodivergent people may experience certain limitations, but they also have many strengths that can be fostered and harnessed for good. Neurodivergent individuals—including Steve Jobs, Bill Gates, and Albert Einstein—are capable of thinking about the world untethered from typical social constructs and seeing solutions others might not consider.

"Everyone is to some extent differently-abled because we are all born different and raised differently. Our ways of thinking result from both our inherent *machinery* and the experiences that have *programmed* us," wrote Robert Austin and Gary Pisano.[8]

This diversity is a wonderful thing.

If it weren't for such diversity of thought and experience, we would understand much less about the world and how to solve problems. Through the eyes of neurodivergent people, we see beyond typical social constructs and uncover new ways of creating.

Thanks to social media and the rise of advocates who are raising awareness for mental health conditions and neurodivergence, we are hearing from a previously silenced population. Stigma and misunderstanding persist, but visibility has inspired a new understanding of these experiences, which fall under the umbrella of neurodivergence, including autism, ADHD, learning differences, and OCD.

Nowadays, people have more awareness of mental health conditions, especially since the COVID-19 pandemic brought us all face-to-face with what many of us try to avoid… our thoughts.

I spent my youth terrified of mine, racked with shame for nothing more than the noise produced by my neurotic mind. I felt certain Satan himself whispered foul lies in my ears to ensure my eternal downfall. If only I knew then what I know now.

It was prejudice all along.

CHAPTER 6

Wrestle with My Self-Loathing

I was nine years old when I first realized I was queer.

My family and I were on a summer beach vacation in California, a tradition we continue to this day. I don't remember much else about this specific beach trip other than the moment I saw *him*. He was gorgeous, and I didn't quite understand what I was feeling, but it was intense.

He was tall and muscular and wore a cap, sunglasses, and long board shorts. He wrestled around in the water with his two sons, both younger than me. I watched him swing them around, put them on his shoulders, and playfully splash them while they all laughed joyfully.

I badly wanted what I saw. I convinced myself I wanted to become like him: a father with kids.

While I stood in the cool, refreshing water of the Pacific Ocean—waves pushing me to and from—I was totally mesmerized by this handsome dude. We could probably call what I was doing *gawking* because I couldn't take my eyes off him.

When my brother Jake approached to see if I wanted to body surf with him, it startled me. Once out of my trance, I felt shame—not for staring—for something I didn't quite understand. Somehow, I sensed it wasn't acceptable.

While Jake and I waited for the right waves to catch that might carry us all the way to shore—Jake always picked the best waves—my staring turned to furtive glances. With each stolen glance came a growing tightness in my chest, worry about what it could mean, and fear of what it would bring. I wasn't sure why I felt it or even what it was, at least, not then.

It was a fear that haunted me for the next eleven years.

When summer ended, I started fourth grade at Hermosa Vista Elementary School because we had recently moved inside its boundaries. It was there, on the playground, where I first learned what I felt and what it meant. I learned exactly what it would bring.

Loathing.

"You walk like a girl, and I bet you sit when you pee!" the boys chanted while I played on the monkey bars. "You're such a homo!"

I learned I was gay because—among other phrases—that's what boys at school started calling me. They taunted me because of my preference for playing with girls on the playground. Their hatred was palpable. I felt powerless and afraid.

To them, I was an *other*, not human.

Of course I preferred girls. They were nice and gentle. They didn't bully me.

The bullying continued through the end of high school. I second-guessed myself often and feared doing or saying any little thing the bullies might consider "flaming," as they called it. I became preoccupied with how I moved my body, sounded when I spoke, and even how I wrote. Apparently, even my handwriting was "faggy."

I feared whatever might make me a target for even more bullying.

I only cared because these kids frequently reminded me what they thought of me and called me derogatory names often. Once, a boy even came up behind me and thrust himself into me, dared by a group of others.

Only those called such names know what they mean. "I hate you because you are different. You don't deserve equal treatment. You have less value."

I knew every one of my bullies from church. I know they didn't learn to treat me that way there. However, not once did someone who didn't go to my church say or do such things.

For five years, my shame festered, hiding with me in the closet. "It is so hard to overcome this sickness, but I can do it," I wrote in my journal on October 29, 2002.

Later that year, on December 16, I wrote, "I want help right now, but I am not sure how to get it. I have questions about certain things and if they are sins. I feel like they are, but they seem like they shouldn't be. How would someone help me overcome it? I would be so ashamed."

On Christmas, I couldn't bear it on my own any longer, and I decided to crack open that closet door. I was fourteen.

All day, I felt a growing nervousness while I scripted and practiced what I would say to my mom when she came to tuck me into bed that night. Yes, my mom still tucked me in, and I cherished it.

"Mom, I'm gay."
No, it's too definite.

"Mom, I'm attracted to men."
Ew. "Men" sounds too old.

"Mom, I'm attracted to boys."
That seems inappropriate.

"Mom, I'm attracted to guys."
Okay, that will have to do.

When my mom came to my room, the scene turned into something out of a soap opera. I lay there trembling and broke down in one of those dry heaving, snotty cries.

"Mom, I need to tell you something. I think you should sit down."

She sat, alarmed but curious. She's great at maintaining poise.

"What is it, son?" she asked while I hyperventilated, struggling to get out the words.

I was certain I'd have to leave the family. By now, Sunday school made it clear to me that being queer would cause my family's fall from God's eternal grace.

I couldn't bring them all down with me.

"Mom, I'm attracted to guys," I let out and paused for the certain shock and dismay.

To my surprise, it didn't come. She sat and thought for a moment.

Then she dismissed my concerns and explained, "Curiosity like this is normal. It's just a phase. You'll grow out of it."

With that, she gently pushed the closet door closed—like I was little again—and she assured me there were no monsters in there... but I already knew that.

I *was* the monster.

As mentioned in chapter 2, I was raised believing I could communicate with God. I prayed multiple times each day and compulsively took any superstitious wishing opportunity to ensure God would "please, make me straight."

I wished to become straight on all the stars I saw shooting across the sky or coins I threw in a fountain. I wished for it when I blew out birthday candles or held my breath for the entirety of a drive through a tunnel. I begged to be one of the two who got to pull apart the turkey wishbone and was distraught if I didn't get the side that afforded me a wish.

I felt shame when another kid blew out their birthday candles because when they did, I tried to steal their wish to use for my own selfish reasons.

My prayers also filled me with shame. In them, I asked God to change me or, at least, not send me to hell. I'd conclude by pleading, "Since you have to send me to hell, please send my family with me. I don't want to be alone." I didn't fear the eternal damnation I was sure I deserved. It was the thought of eternity without my family.

For years, I fervently prayed, fasted, wished, and read the entire Bible and Book of Mormon—cover to cover—at least twice. I took opportunities to teach the LDS Gospel to others, was the leader of every youth group I was in, and volunteered to give sermons before our congregation.

Despite my efforts, I was unchanged and incredibly discouraged. I assumed it meant I wasn't worthy of God's attention and resigned myself to my fate. That didn't deter me from continuing to do whatever I could to convince God I deserved His grace.

Fast forward to March of 2006, during my senior year of high school. My friend Jay told me about Dane. They graduated together a few years before, and Dane was sent home early from his LDS mission for being gay.

Myspace was fresh at the time, and—lucky for me—Dane had a profile. It didn't hurt that he was super cute. While I wrestled with whether I should message him or not, I'm pretty sure I was vibrating. Ultimately, my curiosity won, I hit send, and then questioned my choice. I both hoped for and feared his response. If he did want to meet, I knew I wouldn't be able to resist.

Dane quickly responded affirmatively, and we arranged a time for him to pick me up. The chemistry was palpable. The night I met him was also the first time I ever lied to my parents, and they knew it.

I was going to hell anyway.

Throughout high school, I dated many girls, but I never felt a single spark. They were all cute, fun girls, and I loved spending time with them and their families. The Law of Chastity was my saving grace. It allowed me to justify never kissing any of them. Kissing a girl didn't feel right.

I kissed Dane the first night we met. Even touching hands sent shivers through my body. It felt natural and right. It was another thing I couldn't resist, and with it, I felt something I never imagined I would feel.

I felt joy.

I felt whole.

My experience with Dane was a departure from what I learned in church. There, they taught me my sexuality was perverse, something unnatural. They said if I didn't suppress it, it would only bring me pain.

Except pain is what I felt doing what they told me was *right*.

It wasn't long before the shame I learned to feel set in. My programming would not permit these new feelings, and cognitive dissonance grew out of the self-loathing religion perpetuated.

I labeled us *deviants* for wanting romantic love. In the name of God, men claiming they spoke through Him convinced me what felt natural was wrong. Dutifully, I ended things with Dane and put the monster back in the closet. Like a good, conscientious Christian, I did what had become an almost weekly ritual—I went to my bishop and repented.

Repentance was supposed to bring peace and make me *at one* with God. Instead, I shut the door on the first real thing I experienced and felt further from God than ever. The emptiness I faced throughout my youth turned to darkness. I got a taste of authenticity, then was crushed by the truth those I love abhorred that part of me and preferred I bury it.

How could I turn off the most joyous piece of me, the only part capable of experiencing the fullness of love? How could that be what the people I love wanted for me?

I recently spoke to my father about it, and he expressed deep sadness. "I truly wish I had a better understanding at that point in time, because I totally believed it was a choice," he said. "I wish somebody who'd been through it could have mentored and helped me understand it."

Prior to my teens, I didn't feel close to my dad. From a young age, he spent weekdays in Washington, DC, serving in Congress. When he was home, he was burned out. The burden of serving the people of Arizona rested on his shoulders until he left Congress when I was twelve.

Things changed the day he learned I was queer, and he gave me the first piece of advice that would protect me from the internal torment I suffered for years. I was fifteen. It marked the beginning of my transition from being a mama's boy to being buddies with my dad.

"It's not your fault you have an attraction to men," he said. "Having the attraction is not a sin. It's only a sin if you act on it. It's okay you're gay. You just can't do gay things."

When I met with my friend Wendy, introduced in chapter 2, I asked why she could rapidly embrace her son's sexuality while many parents never got there. She told me about being left-handed, how her dad believed using the left hand was sinful, and demanded she change her orientation to right-handed.

Wendy had to wear a sock on her left hand to avoid the temptation to use it because the Bible suggested only the wicked and cursed are on the left hand of God. Anytime Wendy cried over failing to become right-handed—certain she'd go to hell—her dad chastised her, "Wendy, try harder. We want you in heaven with us."

If Wendy completed her homework with her left hand because she wanted to play, and it took hours to do it with her right, she'd repent for giving in to her wicked nature.

Her dad might as well have said, "It's not your fault you're left-handed. Being left-handed is not a sin. It's only a sin if you act on it. It's okay you're left-handed. You just can't do left-handed things."

While this may not be the ideal piece of advice to give a young queer kid, it was a total game changer for me. I was certain I'd be damned simply for having the attraction and the thoughts. Learning that was false was revelatory.

All I had to do was not act on it. Suppress it. Give up on the potential for love and romantic or sexual intimacy. I'd have to live and die alone with nothing but the love of God to keep me warm at night.

I was comforted.

Most of us learning Wendy's story would find it silly that her dad believed being left-handed is wicked and required converting to right-handedness. Many of the same people wouldn't question how I was treated growing up, though.

Handedness is an innate characteristic, right? How can someone change the orientation of their hands? Why would they?

They might if they faced condemnation and felt like trash for being that way.

Makes you wonder, no? What if each day of your life, you felt like you were disgusting for a characteristic you had no control over? What if it was the part of you that experiences romantic love? What if others insisted you were a gender you aren't?

Numerous people are often told they aren't the gender they identify with and can only be the gender decided by an obstetrician who looks at their newborn genitalia. Doesn't that seem absurd?

Studies on mental well-being and gender identity reject the notion gender divergence results from pathology.[1] Instead, these studies reveal rigidity around gender, community rejection, and societal discrimination of gender divergence are the problem. Intolerance of gender divergence, persisting from outdated notions, leads to harm committed in the name of suppressing perceived rebellion. Victimization like this is the primary contributor to the development of psychological pathology for LGBTQ+ people, including gender dysphoria.

Most parents begin socializing their children to the gender chosen before their first breath. Children learn various behaviors and preferences that are acceptable or not based on their genitals. This gender stereotyping is the *normal* course society encourages parents to take because of archaic traditions, misinformation, and external pressures. Before the child has even left the womb, the foundation of coerced gender conformity is already laid.[2]

"I don't want to be one with the crowd," I wrote in one emotional journal entry. "I want the crowd to be one with me. My being longs to feel free, not overshadowed by the regulations of the world. 'Let me be me' is my one plea. Instead, I hear the words of God weaponized against His beautiful children."

When others blame God for their prejudice or use His words to validate it, assert homosexuality is a disease, or compare it to pedophilia and bestiality, I hear, "I hate you because you are different."

Whenever religions fight to strip away individual freedoms or ask for donations to take away basic rights in the name of God, I hear, "You don't deserve equal treatment."

Those times it's said LGBTQ+ people will be the destruction of society or are converting their children, when they are the ones using conversion to groom us, I hear, "You have less value."

These pains are why I was quick to begin therapy to *repair* what they told me was a disease. I remember thinking, somehow, I would no longer be broken. The conversion therapist promised he could teach me the steps to recovery and maintaining a *healthy* lifestyle.

Like anyone gaslit to believe they were damaged and in need of saving, I *chose* to try.

CHAPTER 7

Converting Two by Two

"Faggot!"

"Sissy!"

"Queer!"

We shouted, as instructed, at the crying boy while he cowered in the middle of the circle we formed.

I was barely eighteen, and the others were my age or younger. The purpose of this *exercise* was to simulate his trauma from bullying, including by his own father. Our conversion therapist, who is a licensed professional counselor (LPC) to this day, designed the role-play to help the boy break through the binds of his "unwanted same-sex attraction."

At least, that's what the LPC claimed. His family counseling center continues to thrive in Mesa, where I grew up.

I remember a pang of wrenching guilt in my heart and gut while I watched the little bit of light remaining inside the boy fade. The snake oil salesman, hired by our parents, urged us on and told us it was for his own good. I still can't fathom how any healing professional could believe such abuse would be beneficial.

If bullying was a fix, the almost decade of being called things like "homo," "faggot," and "butt muncher" surely would have turned me straight. I trained in human psychological development and lived the experience. I promise, it only harms.

In 2006, I was in my senior year at Mountain View High School and was ready to finish. My dad was the chairman of Arizona's Republican Party. My mom was the president of the Arizona chapter of United Families International (UFI), an organization that made it their mission to block progress for LGBTQ+ rights.

I was out to my parents for about three years. It was the same year Arizona's Proposition 107 would be on the ballot. Prop 107 intended to ban gay marriage, like California's Prop 8. My mom was leading the charge.

Through her work at UFI, my mom encountered the LPC, who professed he could heal the wounds that caused individuals like me to become queer. When our church's president told my parents they needed to talk to me about my romance with Dane, they became desperate, and I became hopeless.

I confessed it to him in confidence and in an effort to repent so I could be righteous enough to serve God on a Mormon mission. After demanding I confess *every* sin I could recall committing from the time I turned eight, he then used it to rationalize why I wasn't good enough to serve God that way.

When they took me to see him, the LPC convinced my parents, like many others before and after, that he had the tools to correct such deviancy. Since he is a fully credentialed practitioner, he also bills insurance, and all my parents had to pay him was a co-pay. He made it too easy and spoke with much authority.

After years of doing what I could to prove I was worthy of change, it wasn't enough. I was twelve or thirteen the first time someone compared me to a pedophile and an alcoholic for nothing more than having romantic and physical attraction to males.

I couldn't think of anything else that would lead to change. That's why when the LPC presented what he called "reparative therapy," I agreed to start.

These days, the LPC only treats those with "unwanted homosexual feelings." For a kid like me, programmed to believe I shouldn't want the feelings by my religion, family, and bullying peers, that wouldn't have made a difference. The overbearing expression of homophobia within my religion made my family and me susceptible to believing the LPC had the answer to overcoming my sexual "cannibalism," as he refers to homosexuality.

Scriptures, like Leviticus 18:22, which are twisted to condemn same-gender love, repeated in my mind ceaselessly. I believed the words of James from the New Testament, "faith without works is dead."[1] Since the ritualistic praying, fasting, wishing, preaching, and scripture studying weren't enough, it seemed I could do more. I supposed God required me to take matters into my own hands, *again*.

The LPC told my parents and me that my father was to blame for his frequent absence due to work travel. According to his theory, that meant I "lacked a sufficient male role model and developed sexualized attachment and eroticized emotions"—an archaic premise.

I barely spoke to my dad for more than a year because of it. It felt like my mom put distance between us to remove any feminine influence. I felt terribly alone and abandoned. His claim further isolated me from my family, driving a wedge between us.

"I am disgusted and expect all others would be too," I wrote in my journal later that year on December 30, 2006. "Everyone else sees a facade. One I wish was real. I feel like the deviant is the real me. Why can't that be fake? I know everyone sins, but I feel different. Through the depression, shame, loneliness, anger, guilt, and emptiness, I still know Satan is lying to me. He says I am not worthy of love, am disgusting, and will never change."

It turns out it wasn't Satan lying to me. It was the LPC... well, and church.

I recently asked my dad what he thought about it all, and he revealed the great pain he experienced during my time undergoing SOGIECE. He also felt defrauded by the LPC, who alleged his own lived experience of becoming straight to make a compelling case for how I became broken.

"What I was worried about more than anything, Matthew," my dad explained, "was your happiness, because I'd been led to believe most gay people were really unhappy with their lives and were really tortured"—something the LPC insisted—"I feared for you. Had I understood what I do now, I would have never consented to allow you to go through conversion therapy. I wish someone had guided us to a *real* therapist who understood these issues and could have gotten us to talk through it."

I had no idea how hurt my dad was by it all. I look back and badly wish we had grown together in the experience rather than apart. I needed him more than ever. Instead, the LPC broke us, claiming, "It gets worse before it gets better," when questioned why my relationship with my dad was strained.

For almost two years, I attended weekly individual sessions, group therapies, and the occasional weekend outing for *masculine bonding* to heal the attachment wounds I was told caused my homosexuality. On a weekend camping excursion, the LPC encouraged me and other boys—some minors—to skinny-dip with him and other adult male *mentors*.

You'd think swimming naked with other dudes would have excited me, but I felt sickened by it. The LPC taunted me to *encourage* me to join. He told the others about the body image issues I revealed to him in a confidential session and said I allowed fear to keep me afflicted by my same-sex attraction. He knew the right things to say to erode my self-esteem and further deepen my shame, this time for not being comfortable skinny-dipping into heterosexual *brotherhood*.

On top of that, I also confided in him my belief God was testing me and gave me these burdens to prepare me for something great. He wondered if it could be preparation for leadership in the ex-gay movement. Ironically, the ex-gay movement accuses the LGBTQ+ community of grooming children in this same way.

The LGBTQ+ community, however, only wants people to feel affirmed in their identities. One group tells people they are whole, seen, loved, and affirmed. The other tells people they are wrong, in need of fixing, and rejects them as they are.

Why are we even having this conversation?

While going through sexual orientation conversion efforts, these types of situations were common. If I didn't believe I was broken before, I felt it drilled into me with every session and every outing.

I saw many others broken down like I was. We all bought the condemning messages about being queer they sold in our homes, churches, schools, communities, and from our political leaders. We believed we were a burden on society, gaslit to think we deserved the abuse we had grown accustomed to in the name of protecting society from us.

The LPC convinced us we were lucky to find him because he could give us the knowledge and tools to make the repairs. When nothing we did or learned from him produced the intended outcomes, he persuaded us to believe we didn't want it or didn't try hard enough. He explained it might not be our fault we were broken, but it was our fault if we gave up on the work.

I only believed there was something to fix because men with authority, like the LPC, convinced me something was wrong with me. He asserted the way I experienced romantic attraction and a desire for love was dangerous and harmful to myself and others. He manipulated my beliefs about myself, ultimately leaving me with the sense I was a pervert for wanting love.

I commonly lamented in my journal, "I hate that I feel this way. I badly want this to be okay. I want to like men and it not be a problem." I couldn't trust my own wants, my own needs, or my own mind. He told me if I succumbed to it, I was taking the easy way out.

He claimed if I chose authenticity, I would feel empty—always trying to fill the emptiness through sexual compulsion and depravity. The LPC told me being gay makes us promiscuous, lusting after the flesh of our own gender—*sexual cannibalism*. When I finally accepted my sexuality, I believed I was only capable of promiscuity because that's what I was taught. These generalizations are wrong. Remember scapegoating?

Mathew Shurka founded Born Perfect, an organization advocating for the end of SOGIECE. His conversion therapist similarly isolated Mathew from family and brainwashed him into feeling broken. Like mine, his practitioner denied the existence of homosexuality.

"There was no such thing as love between two people of the same sex because only people who could create a child know how to experience love," Mathew wrote in an article about his experience. "And these were all coming from men who claimed they were ex-gay themselves, or had their own trauma, or, you know, they say that they had cured themselves and were helping others. And that's when the therapist tells you that you're going to live a loveless, hopeless life, trying to fill a void through sex, which you can never do."[2]

He goes on to detail how the process also tore his family apart, and he felt responsible. Even when his mother expressed her acceptance of his sexuality after seeing the harms incurred—pleading with him to stop—Mathew was not deterred from his mission to become straight because of the practitioner's manipulation.

SOGIECE doesn't only harm those subjected to them, Drs. Judith Glassgold and Caitlin Ryan of the Family Acceptance Project discovered. In one study, they determined families are also negatively impacted via alienation and gaslighting.

"Parents and children may be given inaccurate information about sexual orientation and gender identity," they reported, "and are prevented from receiving affirming interventions that assist parents in supporting their children." They also discovered suicide attempt rates for young people who experienced change efforts at home with a licensed professional or religious leader were triple the rates of LGBTQ+ young people who didn't experience SOGIECE.[3]

Adolescence is a time for identity development, romantic exploration, and community finding. For those of us who go through SOGIECE, including identity rejection at the hands of family and community, our adolescence halts.

Instead of forming our identities, others tell us our innate sense of it is wrong. Rather than being free to experience romance, they tell us the natural way of our orientation is dirty, deviant, and abominable. In place of finding community, we face isolation, rejection, and abandonment at the behest of authority figures who say we can't be trusted to do so.

These behaviors erode a person's ego, self-worth, and capacity to know who they are and feel safe in their own bodies and in the world. I personally met with and interviewed Dr. Ryan, who said, "[SOGIECE] is done in a variety of different ways that are so widespread you don't even see them. For example, they might include aspects of neglect or ridicule, along with not letting them have a certain hairstyle.

"People may not see that as a *biggie* or whatever, but these things are so widespread that nobody's thinking about them. For the child, they're giving them the message, 'This part of yourself is bad, damaged, harmful, et cetera.' That's the definition of psychological maltreatment, regardless of the intent," Ryan continued. "Those behaviors can be traumatic for LGBTQ+ people and have a huge impact over the life course, especially if they're not addressed. When they're combined with external change efforts, they're even worse, but of their own accord, they're quite debilitating."

While advocating at the United Nations Human Rights Council for the end of SOGIECE worldwide, the attorney Victor Madrigal-Borloz shared the UN's definition of torture: "Any act by which severe pain or suffering, whether physical or mental, is intentionally inflicted on a person for such purposes as… intimidating or coercing him or a third person, or for any reason based on discrimination of any kind."[4]

Madrigal-Borloz asserts these conversion practices are torture because "they often lead to pain and suffering that will last far beyond their occurrence, leaving indelible scars on a person's body and mind. The combined effects of feeling powerless and extreme humiliation generate profound feelings of shame, guilt, self-disgust, and worthlessness, which can result in a damaged self-concept and enduring personality changes."[5]

We traumatized individuals experience chronic shame, self-doubt and loathing, distrust of others, difficulty forming relationships, hypersensitivity to rejection, and frequently triggered fears of abandonment. We can't even turn to the people who should be there when no one else is.

When we are young kids, our adolescence is robbed from us. It's no wonder why most of the approximately 700,000 individuals who have suffered through the practice become depressed, suicidal, addicted to substances, exploited, or die by suicide.[6]

Others beat us down and break us until we can't even trust our own instincts, feelings, and beliefs about the world and how we fit into it.

This is a global problem. While I write this, only twenty-six of 195 countries across the world have implemented bans on its practice. Only eleven of them ban SOGIECE outright for any person. The rest only ban it for minors.

In the United States, no state bans the practice outright. Young people can still be legally subjected to this psychological torture at the hands of licensed professionals in twenty-three states, and another five states only partially ban it.[7]

In my home state of Arizona, only State Agencies are restricted from using "State and Federal resources to promote, support, or enable" SOGIECE and must have policies "to protect LGBTQ+ minors" from its practice.[8] While a move in the right direction, the law does not prohibit the practice or establish punishments for perpetrators of it.

Even with enacted legal bans, they only protect minors. Young adults and their families, like in my case, are still susceptible to the manipulative, false promises of these practitioners. Legal bans do not block religious practitioners from perpetrating these efforts either, even on children.

In some states, politicians will even claim abusing children in this way is a religious freedom needing protection. I can't highlight this enough.

The excessive mental and emotional burden the practice of SOGIECE places on young people isn't enough for United States lawmakers to put an end to it. To demonstrate the burden of SOGIECE in a manner they can understand and *maybe* deem worth their effort to address, economists calculated the national humanistic burden.

Their study concluded that the United States alone spends an estimated $650 million each year on SOGIECE, including from insurance reimbursements. The harms associated with SOGIECE cost another $8.58 billion per year, putting the total economic burden of SOGIECE at $9.23 billion annually in the United States.[9]

Dr. Johanna Olson-Kennedy, medical director of the Center for Transyouth Health and Development at Children's Hospital Los Angeles, expressed her frustration with this reality. "The human toll is simply not enough to eradicate the dangerous practice of forcing individuals to conform to the heterosexual and cisgender normative expectation," she said.[10]

As long as we continue to perpetuate the belief that LGBTQ+ identities are wrong, abnormal, or sinful, children will continue to die or want to die, become displaced from their homes, dependent on substances, or otherwise burdened by mental health issues.

These costs are far too great.

How will this minority cause the downfall of society? Can we stop telling others how they can live their lives and who they can live them with? Why do we beat them down when all they request is respect?

As loved ones, leaders, and shepherds of these kids, it is our job to protect, support, and lead them on a journey to embrace who they are, not diminish it.

PART III
EVOLUTION

CHAPTER 8
Finding Paradise

Brené Brown, in her book *Braving the Wilderness: The Quest for True Belonging and the Courage to Stand Alone*, said, "True belonging is the spiritual practice of believing in and belonging to yourself so deeply that you can share your most authentic self with the world and find sacredness in both being a part of something and standing alone in the wilderness. True belonging doesn't require you to *change* who you are; it requires you to *be* who you are."[1]

Let me tell you about the time I chose to stand alone in the wilderness.

Before my twentieth birthday, I was dating a young woman named Katelyn. Katelyn was chill and fun. She was also super cute. Katelyn taught me how to kiss, and I enjoyed kissing her. I told myself if I *had* to marry a woman, Katelyn was the one.

If that statement doesn't make you uncomfortable, read it again, *slower this time*.

One day, she texted me, "Matt, we need to talk. Can I come over?"

Prior to texting me, she was in Salt Lake City, Utah, for the Mormon General Conference, a biannual conference broadcast worldwide, where church executives speak to Mormons of the world. While Katelyn was there, she had a spiritual experience. When she told me about it, tears streamed down her face. Her voice cracked and wavered.

"Matt, I don't want to do this, but while I was at the conference, the Holy Spirit told me we can't be together. I have no idea why, and it's not what I want, but I have to trust and listen to it."

She didn't know why, but I did. If ever God gave me a sign, it was this moment.

I was still meeting with the LPC, who was trying to convert me to heterosexuality, a little over a year and a half from when I started. He made it clear I would wrestle with my "unwanted feelings" for life and would have to diligently commit to forever siphoning hetero-masculine energy to fill the emptiness left by my father's absence in my early years.

With Katelyn's revelation, I found myself wondering, *Do I actually not want these feelings, or is it others telling me I shouldn't want them?*

As I thought about it, my thoughts turned to Eve.

God told Adam and Eve, "But of the tree of the knowledge of good and evil, thou shalt not eat of it: for in the day that thou eatest thereof thou shalt surely die."[2] Mormons believe

He meant they'd become mortal and eventually die. They also believe because Adam and Eve weren't mortal, they couldn't honor the only other commandment He gave them: "Be fruitful, and multiply, and replenish the earth."[3]

God gave them an impossible problem to solve. He gave them two conflicting commands, which they couldn't honor simultaneously.

If you ask me, Eve was a pioneer. She knew to give birth to humanity she had to eat from "the tree of the knowledge of good and evil" and become mortal. Then, she could multiply.

Growing up, I identified with Eve.

I, too, had impossible challenges and opposing commands. First, raise a family with a partner I would love for eternity. Second, never eat of the forbidden fruit—pun intended—or I would surely die a spiritual death.

It caused me much suffering. I could never create a family with a partner I *would* love for eternity because I was forbidden from doing it with someone I *could* love for eternity.

One day thereafter, I was in one of the labs I worked at while attending Arizona State University. Appropriately, it was a lab that studied anxiety disorders in children. I was there mindlessly plugging data we collected into the computer, lost in my thoughts since the repetitive task didn't require much focus. When I did, I recalled a time my sister Katie sought counsel from our parents due to confusion and distress over God not answering her prayers.

I remembered my surprised when they told her, "Katie, maybe God doesn't care what you do." I was in the other room, but my ears perked up. This bewildered Katie, and she questioned how that could be.

"Maybe both choices are good," they responded. "Sometimes you have to tell God what you are going to do and have faith He will let you know if you are on the wrong path."

I was alone that day in the psychology lab. I locked the door, turned down the lights, and knelt with a new resolve. I hoped if I was ever going to connect with God, this would be the time. After years of begging God to make me straight, He ended the one straight relationship I thought I could make work.

"Heavenly Father, we need to talk," I prayed aloud. "I'm done asking you to make me straight. I am gay and am going to live my life authentically. If you have a problem with that, you can tell me directly."

No sooner than I spoke those words, a flood of the most intense feelings of love, warmth, and peace washed over me. I felt like someone held me in a powerful, warm embrace, much like being a toddler wrapped in that big, comfy bath towel on my mom's lap. I hadn't felt anything like it before, and I knew it was good.

Love for myself completely overcame me, and I hoped it would never end. Tears streamed down my face, and I held onto the feeling till I no longer could.

I knew then *love is God*.

After what felt like hours and the feeling subsided, I collected myself in that quiet lab—my temple—vocalized my deep gratitude, and set out on my new path. I felt joy and appreciation for all the times throughout my youth when my dad reminded me to trust my connection to God.

To this day, God never disagreed.

Others tried to tear down my experience. When I recounted the details of my rebirth, they diminished it and told me, "Satan is the great deceiver." They refused to accept God would embrace all my parts, even the ones they viewed with disdain. If they were right, it meant God was the misery I felt for all my youth, and Satan was the greatest joy I had ever known.

Dustin Lance Black, one of the great catalysts for marriage equality in the United States, tells a similar story of self-acceptance in his book, *Mama's Boy: A Story from Our Americas*. Black's self-acceptance only came after he felt God gave him permission.

"Still on my knees in prayer, I grew silent and listened… Because if there really was a God, I felt sure He could speak to a far deeper place than my crinkled-up ears," he wrote. "And that night, I thought I felt some sort of God whisper to me, 'I am love.' And so… I chose love."[4]

Like Black and many others, I spent more than a decade hating myself because of the gender of the person I'd someday love and want to share life. I spent years following the *right path*, begging God to change me while He forsook me, and grew certain I'd be damned for all eternity.

Through prayer, I realized all the time I spent doing what authority figures told me was *correct* and fearing hell, I was already in it. Only by embracing my queer self did I find salvation.

Just like God cast Eve out of the Garden, my community cast me out, othering me because I ate the forbidden fruit.

The irony is the Garden was my true hell. Only after they cast me out did I find paradise.

Once cast out, I gained the knowledge of good and evil and experienced true growth. I learned the difference between unconditional love the way God intended it and love like men professed, who claimed they were His mouthpiece.

I understood that to find love, I would have to do like Eve: break one commandment to honor another. I never looked back.

I looked forward and accepted the risk I took when I left what I knew and chose to stand alone in the wilderness.

Arriving at this position did not mean I stopped experiencing negative thoughts about myself. I still have to sort through the aftermath of years of being rejected for a core piece of my identity. Because of it, I will probably forever have a mind that tells me I am unworthy of love in situations that remind me of past rejection.

The LPC assured me I would spend my life trying to fill a void. It's no wonder, since he worked to convince me I was deficient and created the void he claimed was there all along.

That's trauma, not truth.

According to Drs. Shelley Carson and Ellen Langer from Harvard University, "One important aspect of self-acceptance is the ability and willingness to let others see one's true self."[5] Real therapy moves you toward this ideal.

By leaning into the values from my upbringing of love, respect, personal responsibility, growth, and standing up for what is right, I learned to embrace my whole self over time. Without these values, the process would have been much more difficult.

Carson and Langer go on to say, "Accepting responsibility for one's private world is part of self-acceptance. Change is possible only when one mindfully embraces both the responsibilities and the opportunities of the decisions they have made."[6]

I grew to understand the pain of my youth wasn't my fault, but it was my responsibility to heal and ensure it didn't overshadow my present and future.

You might notice the parallel between this and what the LPC told me about becoming straight. It's quite common for psychological manipulators to twist healthy concepts to groom others. The key difference here is the outcome. One harms while the other heals.

My friend and author of *Love Is the Path*, Claudia Cardozo, told me a bit about her own story of self-acceptance. "Most of my life, I lived like I wasn't good enough, like I always fell short of my own expectations. That narrative was exhausting."

Like I did, Claudia realized she had to let go. "Because to be bold, you have to detach from what other people think of you," she said. "The people who truly accept you are the people who matter."

For those working toward self-acceptance, it's important to realize we each have great power in our own lives and can make that choice. If we can't accept ourselves because our behaviors are not in line with our values, we can make other choices. We can choose other values.

We can also choose how we view ourselves and our situation. We can decide we have innate self-worth and can learn and grow from our mistakes and adversity. Carson and Langer say we do this by recognizing we are all "multifaceted individuals whose potential is limited only by [our] limited perspectives."[7]

One of the most difficult parts of embracing ourselves is accepting the parts we like least. Many challenge the notion of self-acceptance, believing we shouldn't accept the parts we want to change.

"The curious paradox is that when I accept myself just as I am, then I change," said Carl Rogers, a famous psychologist and founder of humanistic psychology.[8]

Why accept something you want to change, though?

It's easy to confuse acceptance with resignation. Resignation involves giving up and giving in. Acceptance requires us to decide we have worth, regardless of the characteristics we want to change. When we refuse to accept our whole selves, we look at these parts with disdain or avoid looking at them at all.

Through his work with parents and children, Rogers developed his theory of unconditional positive regard or belief we learn best through unconditional acceptance and understanding. This is the belief that nothing a person is or does diminishes their value or humanity.[9]

My brother Jake modeled this while we vacationed with our family—remember, he always finds the upside. His son was in a time-out, which Jake kept extending because his son would not adjust his behavior. With compassion, Jake expressed to me, "He is so stubborn. It's a wonderful quality and could be such a great strength if he can learn to channel it in the right way."

Like Jake, try to find the upside to the qualities you may dislike. Maybe you don't need to change it. Maybe, like Jake says, you need to "channel it in the right way."

In either situation, if we don't acknowledge and accept these parts, we can't realistically understand them to effectively grow. We need to stop seeing ourselves through a lens of deficit and see opportunities within ourselves for growth.

This reminds me of a story my friend Steve May told me. Steve was a member of the Arizona House of Representatives and has worn many hats, including a seat on the board of one•n•ten, a social service agency for LGBTQ+ youth in

Arizona. It was "one of the stories that truly crushed me when I was at one•n•ten," he said, his eyes looking down at his desk.

He told me about a mother who spoke of her child who committed suicide. The mother expressed comfort in knowing her transgender child "knew we loved her, but she also knew she'd never be accepted in the world."

"We've got to teach people you don't need to be accepted by the world," Steve's voice escalated as he spoke, and his gestures broadened emphatically.

In a society that values conformity over self-acceptance, all too often, the cost is life. At best, the cost is poor self-esteem.

When these are the costs, why not accept things you want to change?

Lady Gaga is a strong advocate for self-acceptance and a role model for authenticity. She urges a move toward a better society. She understands embracing oneself is to "celebrate all the things they don't like about themselves... and to be truly happy from the inside."[10]

Gaga experienced significant bullying growing up, especially for her looks. She learned self-acceptance means recognizing that "I have the ability and the free will to choose the way the world will envision me."[11]

According to Gaga, self-acceptance involves taking control of your narrative and deciding how the world will see you. It's about standing in your truth, even when faced with criticism or rejection. It's about asserting you are enough while still embracing the potential for growth and transformation.

If I learned anything from my experience, it's that growth doesn't come without pain. My pain began when I realized I had a quality others viewed with disdain. Like the kid from Steve's story, I was too concerned with the opinions of others.

How could I not be?

Most people around me shared these harmful beliefs. No safe space existed for me. I didn't belong anywhere and allowed myself to believe the messages of intolerance I heard across all spaces I lived: home, church, school, community, and in the laws meant to protect me.

Others accepted me because I hadn't revealed my truth. Through experience, I learned that in order to embrace myself, I had to lose the false approval of others. Once I did, I realized I didn't need anyone else's acceptance because I belonged to myself.

"I finally embraced in myself what I tried to push away and felt shame for so long," I proclaimed in my journal one day after my talk with God. "I am homosexual, and though I am still afraid, I am not ashamed. One thing to remember: Do not hold on to the bitterness and hate. Embrace those with whom you fought. Forgive them with repentant actions, yourself."

Harmful rhetoric and misinformation caused my family to confuse my tendency to defy *norms* with rebellion. All I wanted was to feel whole, seen, and loved for being me, but they felt they needed to suppress what they didn't understand.

More people each day are courageously owning their differences despite the risks involved. These individuals not only embrace their diverse qualities; they also channel them toward progress by celebrating the strengths these unique attributes confer.

Alok Menon, a queer author, comedian, and advocate, beautifully describes this movement toward authenticity and self-acceptance. Speaking on *The Man Enough* podcast, they eloquently captured a profound truth.

"People have been taught to fear the very things that have the potential to set them free. They don't know how to feel love, like we can give," Menon explained. "That's why marginalized communities are persecuted. It's because of the presence of love that people feel they can't inherit on this earth. What we, as transgender and nonconforming people, said is, 'There's a wound here, and I'm going to commit my life to realign my spiritual core such that I never have to compromise myself for other people's love. I'm going to prioritize and choose me in a world that makes me have to contour myself into someone else's fiction.'"[12]

Menon's words resonate deeply with the journey many of us in the LGBTQ+ community undertake; a journey marked by the decision to prioritize our truth over the demands of a world that expects us to conform to its fiction. This choice, though it may feel isolating at first, is part of a broader, inspiring movement.

Even with the increasingly visible hatred toward LGBTQ+ people, more individuals proudly own their authenticity in the face of certain backlash. When we choose authenticity, we not only find freedom for ourselves but also give others the permission and courage to do the same.

That's a testament that love matters more.

From the mouth of the goddess RuPaul herself: "If you can't love yourself, how in the hell you gonna love somebody else? Can I get an amen?"[13]

CHAPTER 9
Love Thy Neighbor

Growing up I was taught the highest law, second only to love for God, is, "Love thy neighbor as thyself."[1]

That means not loving others is one of the greatest sins, no?

Those of us who face intolerance know the pain of rejection and being cast into the wilderness to fend for ourselves. Many who survive the journey arrive at the other side with a deep understanding of what it means to suffer the sins of the world—reborn with the capacity to hold empathy and forgiveness for ourselves and others.

Even with the pain of rejection because of it, I consider my queerness a gift because it inspired my evolution from suppressing and hating my stigmatized parts to fully embracing them. Once able to do that for myself, celebrating the differences I encountered in others was an easy next step.

As I mentioned in chapter 8, the process can be lonely because those around you might not know how to do the same. For many, some loved ones won't embrace them.

I prepared myself for such an outcome. While I knew I could enjoy a wonderful life by embracing myself, even if my family never celebrated with me, I still wanted them to change, badly.

Early after I began living authentically, I frequently rebuked my family for not accepting me and demanded they change their long-held, deeply ingrained beliefs. What I didn't understand was my family *did* accept me. They considered me part of their *us* even though they regarded my community—other LGBTQ+ people—as *them*. They accepted I was queer, but it had no impact on their beliefs about others they considered outsiders.

This is a common misunderstanding. People think acceptance is enough, but it's not. Eventually, I realized it wasn't my family's acceptance I wanted. Sure, it was better than intolerance, but it was insufficient. What I actually wanted was for them to embrace me fully and celebrate this core piece of me—the greatest catalyst for the human I evolved into.

We all contain a multitude of diverse parts. We might dislike some of the parts, but we have to permit ourselves to embrace them all. The process for embracing others is the same. I disliked parts of my family members, like their religious and political identities, but I had to let go of demanding they change.

Most people think the ability to change another's mind is a strength, but true strength is the willingness to change our own.

I decided to embrace my family even though they hadn't done the same for me. I loved them despite their beliefs, which denied my right to "Life, Liberty, and the pursuit of Happiness."

It was painful.

I had to lean into my inner belonging and recognize while our religion programmed us similarly, how we experienced the world around us and our responses to it were quite different. My family did not have the experience of being condemned for existing and, therefore, couldn't see the harm.

Embracing my family required I drastically challenge my own beliefs and those of others who said they were "bad" or "ignorant" for not readily adopting my views. I also had to have self-compassion and let go of the criticizing expressions of my mind: *I must not be important enough. They believe I don't deserve happiness. I am unlovable.*

Once I allowed myself to feel the sadness and stop judging myself for their choices, I recognized their choices represented their own limitations and not my worth. Then, I connected with them.

When I did, they got to know the real me. In doing so, they began to celebrate the real me.

While vacationing with my family recently, my sister Lara apologized for the pain I experienced because of the family's mistakes along their journey toward embracing me fully. She said, "I'm glad you are in our lives and the lives of my children because it's taught us how to truly love and accept others."

Lara's recognition and expression of her gratitude indicated she saw and understood my suffering. Like the songs she'd sing to soothe my distress because our mom was late, her words were music to my ears.

Like with my family, "much of learned information has been imparted by an authority figure or has been presented in absolute language," according to psychologists Carson and Langer. "Individuals often accept this information mindlessly and become trapped within a single perspective, oblivious to other ways of seeing the information."[2]

I recently had a conversation with a devout Christian man who questioned my faith in humanity and desire for the meeting of basic needs for all people. He espoused a belief I heard before but hadn't encountered in some time.

Leaning close, with wide eyes, he mocked incredulously, "Oh God, you want world peace?" He then insisted, "That will never be possible. Humans are inherently evil," and refused to accept my understanding, which was contrary to his.

I stood there—dumbfounded—wondering how someone who believes God created humans in His image could contend they are evil.

The trouble with this type of thinking is its foundation in an immature defense mechanism called projection. Projection occurs when we attribute feelings or urges we believe are unacceptable or immoral to others to avoid confronting them in ourselves. It's also one of the roots of othering. Without introspection and self-awareness, projection easily affects what we believe about others and how we treat them.

Projection of this type will lead a person, like the man I mentioned, to unconsciously think, *If there is evil in me, others must be worse.*

If you're in need of a good antidote, Dr. Kristin Neff recommends practicing self-compassion. It "recognizes that all individuals should be treated with kindness and caring and that a compassionate attitude toward oneself is needed to avoid falsely separating oneself from the rest of humanity."[3]

Through mindful self-awareness, I catch many of my own projections because none of us are immune to them. It's upsetting, but I must remind myself these projections are the product of my animalistic brain and of being brought up in a society that believes there is a default or *normal* way to be.

Even though I work to challenge gender norms, I often catch myself thinking in gendered terms or assuming the gender of somebody I have never spoken to. I have to remind myself neither their gender nor what's in their pants has any bearing on my life, how I will treat them, or if I will respect them.

It comforts me to remember the automatic thought that pops into my head does not represent my character. It's the thoughts and actions that follow that define me. If it weren't for my process of self-acceptance, which involved overcoming the prejudice I internalized toward my sexuality, I probably wouldn't have developed the capacity to do the same for others.

In chapter 4, I mentioned Leandra Stanley, who self-identifies as an "unapologetic, fat, Black, disabled queer" on her LinkedIn profile.[4] Even with multiple intersecting identities, Leandra had her own painful process of learning to embrace the diversity within herself and others.

When I spoke with Leandra, she offered a challenge for beginning this process of growth. "If you really care about others, it's important you care about their humanity, their equal rights, and equity in accessing them. There's always room for growth. I wasn't always as *woke* as I am now. It took a lot to get here."

She continued by offering compassion, "It can be baby steps, but you have to be willing to look your biases in the face and not turn away from the ways you might have oppressed others in the past, or even now."

Recognizing the universal nature of human failing, Leandra emphasized our shared humanity, reminding us to have self-compassion because "we are all going to keep messing up."

My family's process to overcome their misinformed beliefs about my and other LGBTQ+ identities was incremental, as Leandra mentioned it could be. My dad explained his original resistance to my being queer stemmed from his belief I *chose* it to defy them. That changed one day during a conversation we had, which opened his eyes.

"I remember saying something about the choices you make, and you got really emotional," he said.

Even now, as I recall the conversation, I feel the punch in my gut at his words. It solidified for me that I was alone and unseen all the years I languished because of a quality I could no more control than my hair color or hand orientation.

I couldn't believe after years of emotional torment, bullying, and rejection, he could even consider I chose something that would bring all that suffering upon myself.

"Dad, do you honestly think if all that was a choice, I would have chosen it?" I asked, each word more painful than the last.

These days, he understands "being gay is part of who you are, and I love who you are," he told me. "I believe you were born this way. If God doesn't love you for the way He made you, then He isn't a God I believe in."

While LGBTQ+ identities are typically not by choice, even if they were, it shouldn't matter. What's wrong with celebrating people for living their lives in whatever way feels right for them, and affords them joy in this life, when they aren't harming others?

How does affirming someone's authenticity hurt anyone?

It's expected we embrace people for chosen identities like religion and political party, notwithstanding the damages they caused throughout history. Why are innate identities treated differently?

People commonly only undertake this process of reflection and belief changing when faced with an important catalyst like my queerness was for my family and me.

"You are your family's most important teacher. You are teaching them by being your authentic self," Wendy, whom I introduced in chapter 2, expressed with pride beaming in her eyes. With four queer children out of five, she's experienced it firsthand.

"In churches, you are showing us what it is to love the way Christ taught us to love. And it's not in the judgmental way they're doing now. It's really beautiful, and it's an unfair burden, but it's also strength and resilience," Wendy voiced reverently. "I fully believe straight people are boring, and we're gray. You guys are the color, and I'm not even trying to make a rainbow reference."

Wendy's words, while they highlight the contrast she perceives between straight and queer identities, speak to a larger idea.

The notion of a default identity is widespread across cultures, though it varies depending on where you are. Across the world, most cultures assume the default sexual orientation is straight, and anything else is a deviation from the *norm*. In the United States, the common presumption is that White is the default racial identity.

Such thinking neglects the history of the world and fails to recognize diversity *is* the default. Variation is the norm, not the exception.

It's quite silly when you consider White people make up less than 20 percent of the world's population, and that's generous. According to Ipsos, a global market research firm, they estimate 20 percent of the world's population does not identify as heterosexual. That doesn't even include transgender and nonbinary-identified people.[5]

By that accounting, queer people outnumber White people. It seems, therefore, being White is more *abnormal* than being queer.

Once we can celebrate all our parts, why wouldn't we do the same for others?

When we reject parts of our collective whole, we miss out on the fullness of life, the capacity to evolve, and the beauty around us.

In the documentary *Mama's Boy*, about his mother Anne's life, Dustin Lance Black recounts her defiance of norms and belief in and capacity to open up to the goodness of others. He outlines how Anne embodied this process.

Anne was paralyzed from the waist down. Doctors and other authorities told her she wouldn't amount to much. She knew what it was like to be cast out rather than celebrated for her strengths and differences and left behind a legacy of healing division through compassion and curiosity.

"She showed the curiosity to listen more than she spoke. My mom believed it was incredibly important to keep relationships together, to keep friendships together, communities and country together," Black said. "Courage… curiosity… bridge building. That was my mom."[6]

She understood what research now validates. According to the US Surgeon General Dr. Vivek Murthy, "Social connection is a fundamental human need, as essential to survival as food, water, and shelter. Throughout history, our ability to rely on one another has been crucial to survival. Now, even in modern times, we human beings are biologically wired for social connection."[7]

Since "half of US adults report experiencing loneliness, with some of the highest rates among young adults," Dr. Murthy made it his mission to reduce the burden of loneliness in the United States and advocate for increasing social connectedness.[8]

He recognizes advancing social connection can't be done in isolation, and it isn't accessible to everyone. "That is partially because we need others to connect with, but also because our society plays a role in either facilitating or hindering social connection," Dr. Murthy notes.[9]

Those most impacted by loneliness are the most vulnerable in society, including the marginalized and those with less power, like racialized and the LGBTQ+ community.

Many believe they can avoid this by following the Golden Rule, "Do unto others as you would have them do unto you," but this is a flawed concept.

As individuals, we carry a myopic view of reality developed through our singular experience and colored by our thoughts, emotions, and biases. While others may walk a similar path through life, no two people share the same makeup or journey.

Imagine two people from different cultures meeting for the first time. One of them comes from a culture that believes eye contact is polite, while the other comes from a culture where they consider eye contact aggressive and confrontational.

Who is right?

If you come from a culture in which eye contact is polite, should you follow the Golden Rule and make eye contact with them since that's the treatment you want? Should you assume they are rude if they don't make eye contact?

If we treat others the way we want to be treated, we completely neglect their preferences and opinions for how to engage with them. Carson and Langer call this stance "mindlessness" and suggest it "pigeonholes experiences, behaviors, objects, and other people into rigid categories."[10]

I propose an evolved alternative: "Do unto others as *they* prefer you do unto *them*."

How can we know another's preferences? "Courage... curiosity... bridge building."

Talk to them. Ask them. Simply recognize others think and believe differently than you and take an interest in learning how to see the world as they do.

It's daunting to imagine doing for every action we take, which could affect another person. That's not necessary, however. It's important to consider in situations that carry greater importance and adjust when someone reflects a preferred alternative to the action we took, like when they reflect a name or pronoun of their preference.

When we adopt a mindset of curiosity and understanding, accepting others have different experiences, we will move about the world with more compassion and empathy for others.

Daryl Davis is a Black musician who wanted to learn from members of the Ku Klux Klan why they have the beliefs they do. He modeled humility and curiosity for others' perspectives. In a TEDx Talk, he shared his story of becoming friends with one of the Klan's national leaders, highlighting the importance of listening to others' stories.

"Respect is the key," Davis insisted. "Sitting down and talking—not necessarily agreeing—but respecting each other to air their points of view. Because of that respect and my willingness to listen, and his willingness to listen to me, he ended up leaving the Klan. And there's his robe right there. I am a musician, not a psychologist or sociologist. If I can do that, anybody in here can do that."[11]

While extreme, it's a great example of someone putting their faith in common humanity. It illustrates the capacity to reflect and change when presented with an alternative narrative to what one calls truth. Davis demonstrates the absolute power of courage, curiosity, and bridge building.

To celebrate diversity or not is a choice. It's a choice to embrace the beauty in color. It's a choice to value the strength in difference. It's a choice to consider all humans worthy even when their values are not in line with your own.

What choice will you make?

CHAPTER 10
Returning to the Cave

John Stuart Mill, a philosopher and member of Parliament of the United Kingdom, spoke at the University of St. Andrews in Scotland on February 1, 1867. He said, "Bad men need nothing more to compass their ends, than that good men should look on and do nothing... because he will not trouble himself to use his mind on the subject."[1]

It isn't enough to simply agree injustice should not occur. Injustice will persist while good people do nothing more than send thoughts and prayers to those who experience it.

Like many who experienced mistreatment from a young age because others considered me *different*, I became intimately familiar with injustice. I made it my mission to raise awareness and promote fairness for all.

"No pride for some of us without liberation for all of us," a vision attributed to Marsha P. Johnson and Sylvia Rivera—according to Micah Bazant—which I made my own.[2] I recognized if I deserve to have my humanity affirmed, all people, even those different from me, are entitled to the same.

Others have reduced me to a slur and shamed me for being myself. Members of my community are beaten and murdered for living authentically, and many Christians wage a culture war against us. I experienced psychological torture through SOGIECE and manipulation to believe I was broken. Then I looked around and saw this sort of injustice happening everywhere. Because I lived the experience, I could see how it impacted others.

Those who fit the *norm* are unlikely to experience this burden, which makes it challenging to adopt a perspective or see a need for change. To those in that position: it's not your fault.

Choosing to be willing *is* your responsibility, however.

It takes a willingness to open your mind, listen to, and believe the stories of others' lived experiences, even when they don't align with your own.

In his "Allegory of the Cave," Plato does an awesome job describing the process of moral evolution and developing awareness through symbolism.[3] He tells of people held captive in a cave from birth, bound in such a way they can only see the wall in front of them. Behind them is a path that free people walk along. Beyond the path, a fire sits on a ledge above. The fire casts shadows of the free people, walking along the path, onto the wall in front of the captives.

These individuals cannot see anything other than the wall and shadows cast by the fire upon it. They have never known anything else and come to believe this is reality. They don't even know to want for more. They grow comfortable, trusting there is nothing else. Ultimately, they make sense of the world, how they can, from what they observe.

On occasion, an individual escapes their binds and begins to explore the cave. When they discover an opening to the cave, they venture toward it. The light of the sun outside becomes brighter and brighter, requiring their eyes time to adjust. Once outside and their eyes have adjusted, they see paradise and want to share it with people they care about back inside.

When they share this wonderful news, they are met with different reactions. Several resist the information with disbelief, reluctant because they believe inside the cave is their garden, and doubt real paradise is outside. They may have grown too comfortable with what they know and fear what they don't. It may take more time to process and adjust to everything.

Others prefer to stay in the cave, even with evidence of what's outside. Maybe it feels safer and easier to deal with the limits and security the cave provides, whereas what lies beyond is full of unknowns. Many accept the information easily and are grateful to have their eyes opened to the beauty of paradise.

We are all born with limitations. We grow to see the world through the eyes of those who raise us and anyone involved in teaching us how to apply meaning to what we experience. Over time, we encounter more people who might impart their view of the world if we are open to receiving it.

Some of us either don't encounter others who are different or might not be open to seeing the world like others experience it. Those of us prefer the comfort of *tradition*.

Lack of exposure to others or unwillingness to be open might affirm the way we see the world is the only way to observe it. Discomfort with the unknown, fear of what we believe is beyond the cave, or preference to keep things simple may fuel our hesitance to challenge ourselves and grow our insights about the world.

Many of us will readily embrace the world beyond the cave, beyond the boundaries of the cultures, religions, and communities we grew up in. We come to see the world through the eyes of all those with whom we've shared experiences and stories. We live life in a way that is full and real because we recognize every individual perceives reality through their own lens.

We learn the more lenses you view the world with, the better you see reality. Through this process, we gain perspective and the capacity to see beauty all around. We can be grateful for the limited view we grew up with because it got us to where we are and can want those we love, who may still look through one low-powered lens, to see much more.

When we take on the work of sharing this good news, some will hesitate or even resist.

It's easy to forget our eyes are no longer acclimated to the dark when we return to the cave. We must remember how to see like the cave dwellers to connect with those still residing there. "Wherefore each of you, when his turn comes, must go down to the general underground abode and get into the habit of seeing in the dark," Plato explained.[4]

Often, those who leave the cave do it because it doesn't serve them by staying. Like I was in my youth, many are harmed by the binds holding them to that limited existence. They decide the discomfort of staying bound far outweighs the discomfort of the unknown and take the chance.

Being cast out into paradise was an experience I had to share with others, especially my family. It didn't matter how it turned out. I had to try. After years of asking God to send them to hell with me so I wasn't alone, I owed it to them to demonstrate what I had learned. I am one of those called to return to the cave and teach anyone willing to listen.

Marginalized people shouldn't have to pave the way toward greater inclusivity, but it's often the case. We must dig deep, find the willingness and strength within ourselves, and share our stories.

Some experienced too much harm to feel safe going back and doing the work to bring others into the light. Those of us who can will do the work on their behalf.

Being othered isn't necessary to learn what it's like and recognize the injustices that occur. It's up to each of us, regardless of privilege or status, to practice curiosity and respect.

When I expressed my support for my family and their views, many found it unacceptable. I can understand why they thought that. Prior to coming out, my parents played active roles in not only blocking the LGBTQ+ community's access to certain rights but also stripping some away.

I take peace in knowing by the time I chose to embrace my family despite their harmful beliefs, they were no longer involved with any LGBTQ+ opposition. They hadn't evolved to a pro-LGBTQ+ stance, though. That came later.

I chose to support my family because I knew if I wanted them to see things through my lens, I needed to remember what it was like to see in the dark before I could help them acclimate to the bright light beyond the cave. Since embracing my and others' diversity, they have tried to make amends.

My dad lobbied multiple Republican legislators in Arizona to ban SOGIECE and spoke on panels with me about the harms of its practice. When he did, Shannon Minter of the National Center for Lesbian Rights (NCLR) told us my dad was one of the few parents of the numerous conversion therapy survivors Shannon met who was willing to speak out against the practice.

Lara, my oldest sister, recently served on the school board in our hometown, Mesa, Arizona. There, she did what she could to provide a compassionate space for LGBTQ+ students and teachers. On occasion, she received threats of violence from conservative community members, and security had to walk her to and from her car.

Dustin Lance Black, a champion for marriage equality, who wrote the screenplay for *Milk*—the story of Harvey Milk— met with me when I began writing this book. He told me what it was like growing up in a Mormon community where they treated his mom as subhuman for walking with crutches due to her paralysis. He explained her mistreatment, more than any other experience, contributed to his belief that "you should be able to live a life that's filled with happiness, promise, and opportunity, even if you're very, very different from the norm or majority."

Because of his sense of justice, Black gravitated to the story of Harvey Milk. In his documentary *Mama's Boy*, he said, "I heard the story of a man who believed that minorities and disenfranchised folks—including gay people and disabled people—could come together to win more acceptance, to have better lives. And that message gave me hope."[3]

Many believe they have a right to use the government to mandate others live by their restrictive value system. They refuse to allow others the joy they experience living differently.

I met with Neil Giuliano, whom I introduced in chapter 3, to understand his perspective. He said, "Your religion can have whatever laws, rules, sacraments, or whatever you want to have. That's not the government. The government is supposed to treat everybody the same, and it still doesn't."

I asked how he would approach finding common ground on the topic, and he said, "I would ask them to consider their place in society equally to the people they are opposing. Why are they opposing this group of people who are trying to live their lives? Why are they compelled to insert themselves into the desire for happiness of someone else?"

When US Supreme Court Justice Anthony Kennedy gave one of the deciding votes to legalize same-gender marriage, he reflected upon the history of criminalizing same-gender relations in the US. Over eight years ago, he said, "Outlaw to outcast may be a step forward, but it does not achieve the full promise of liberty."[6]

Currently, LGBTQ+ Americans and their allies are outlaws again. On January 3, 2024, the ACLU reported that 510 bills across the country were under consideration that oppose the rights of transgender Americans. These include policies that would make it a crime to provide identity and worth-affirming healthcare to children.[7]

States like my home state of Arizona have many such bills under consideration in their legislatures. One of the bills proposed in Arizona would require school employees to *out* LGBTQ+ students to their parents. Another would make it illegal for a school employee to refer to students how they prefer.

How is it that traditions many Americans cling to and demand we uphold involve criminalizing respect for a child?

"They ask for equal dignity in the eyes of the law. The Constitution grants them that right," Justice Kennedy affirmed.[8]

Many are resistant to progress and allege it harms people without producing clear evidence it does. It seems like, to them, the millions of people harmed by perpetuating these traditions are no more than collateral damage. They resist self-improvement all while recognizing these harms and hold onto the notion "that's just how it's always been done."

How does granting people basic rights or respecting their preferences harm anyone?

Continuing to do things that don't work for all people or are no longer effective simply because "we always have" is unacceptable. My mom reminds me that I had a strong sense of justice and dissatisfaction with hierarchy from a young age.

She remembers numerous calls from the school because I challenged authority in one way or another. One time, in ninth grade, I worked in the school cafeteria, and the manager complained that I refused to obey her orders.

"Did Matthew say why?" my mom asked.

My boss responded, "He said what I told him to do was inefficient and could be done better. He needs to apologize."

My favorite part of the story my mom likes to leave out.

"Well," she paused and asked, "was his way more efficient?"

"That's beside the point," the woman replied. "I'm in charge. He should do it because I said so."

I am grateful for the ways my mom encouraged me not to accept something purely because someone said so.

"I have been thinking about life and fairness," I wrote in my journal around that time. "People often complain life is unfair, then, when they do something unfair, will say, 'I'm sorry, but life is unfair.' I don't understand why people grieve over life being cruel but use the same excuse they hate to hear. If you're upset about the fairness of life, do something about it instead of being unfair to somebody else!"

Life isn't fair, but why would we let that stop us from trying to do better?

Even at fourteen, I knew tradition was harmful and ineffective. I felt constrained by the limitations put upon me by authority figures. Often, these individuals can't or won't accept fairness is possible or that the process for creating it is rooted in equity, because equality isn't enough.

Equality means all people have the same resources and opportunities available to them. Equity recognizes that even though opportunities and resources are available to all, we don't all start from the same place, and not all access opportunities easily.

Through equity, those with reduced ability or access to resources and opportunities might be granted different or additional support to level the playing field. A minority of people might get more of the *pie* because they have a greater need. Some might not get any of the pie because they already have several back home. Others might donate pies because they are pie makers who can produce even more pies than the ones they provide.

People believe equity is unfair because they receive less support than those who are economically insecure. If you want the benefits given to those with less, you also have to live with less.

Remember the rigged game of Monopoly from chapter 4? Or the evolved Golden Rule I mentioned in chapter 9? Treat others according to their preferences and needs.

We must recognize the common humanity shared by all. Each person has value, even if it's not redeemable through capitalism.

Developing this awareness can be difficult. We either experience the pains of living in a woefully misguided society, like I and many marginalized others have, or indirectly through grief over the pain we caused others with our previous beliefs and actions.

Steve May, whom I mentioned in chapter 8, shares my hope for and faith in humanity. "We have to learn how to be brave and kind," he said when I spoke with him. "We're not being either because we aren't engaging people in dialogue. We're ignoring people, shunning people, ridiculing people. We need to learn how to change our behavior. We have to have the conversations. I still believe the American people will get it."

We were all conditioned by a history that pits human against human and group against group. We were sold the lie that to succeed, someone else must fail. That's not the case. We all can succeed. It requires we each do our part to create a world that celebrates diversity and harnesses our differences for the greater good. How we got here isn't our fault, but how we choose to move forward is.

Just like the prisoners in Plato's cave, who escaped and discovered paradise, felt it was their duty to return to the cave, readjust to the darkness, and bring others into the light, we must also. You might not be the type who donates money, testifies before Congress, or speaks out publicly, but we all can change our behavior, speech, and who we let make policies that affect us and millions of our neighbors.

Dr. Vivek Murthy, surgeon general of the United States, said our current *us versus them* mentality has contributed to a crisis of epidemic proportions in the US. In his *Advisory on the Healing Effects of Social Connection and Community*, he writes, "If we fail to [build a more connected society], we will pay an ever-increasing price in the form of our individual and collective health and well-being. We will continue to splinter and divide until we can no longer stand as a community or a country. Instead of coming together to take on the great challenges before us, we will further retreat to our corners—angry, sick, and alone. We are called to build a movement to mend the social fabric of our nation."[9]

When I was in high school, I had a strong orientation for righting wrongs. I wrote this short poem one day while daydreaming about a better world. It still describes my vision:

"If we all relieve one another's burdens,
we could beat anything we face.
To support each other, love everyone,
is not beyond all possible belief.

All it takes is courage and faith.
Of course, it takes willingness too.
Life will be much easier for all,
when we all relieve one another's burdens."

It's important to remember fault doesn't rest with any of us alone, but each one of us can do something to make a difference and improve the problem. It requires we reflect on our own beliefs and evaluate them for unintended biases that easily develop living in our world. We also need to ask ourselves how our beliefs might affect our actions and impact other people.

Don't be good. Be better.

CONCLUSION
Embracing the Journey

"I haven't evolved to that station."

When my dad announced my being gay hadn't changed his belief marriage should be between a man and a woman, it didn't surprise me, but it still crushed me.

I reflected on his words, and a spark of hope grew. *Haven't evolved*—a pair of words that suggested openness to a different state in the future, a willingness to grow and change.

I knew what he suggested and remembered how painful it was to reject the entire foundation of my belief system. I legitimately believed gay thoughts were temptations Satan and his followers whispered into my ears. I was convinced acting on them was a choice because they insisted there was only male and female, only heterosexual love.

It was true my dad hadn't evolved *to that station*, but he was on that journey.

It goes without saying the *station* my family started at was intolerant. I could have gay thoughts, but I couldn't *be* gay. Our religion didn't really promote tolerance with the "hate the sin, love the sinner" mantra. Despite literally everyone *sinning* every day, they seemed to only recite this phrase after matters one only gossips about in a hush.

Why bring hate into it at all? We're all sinners, no? Why not leave it at "love the sinner"?

"Sadly, this fear of difference is our current state of being," Dustin Lance Black writes in his memoir *Mama's Boy*, "despite all the proof that it's our differences that make this world magical, delicious, entertaining, innovating, and downright livable."[1]

I experienced firsthand how hard it is to relinquish a belief, especially since I was absolutely convinced doing so would harm my chance at achieving eternal glory. For those who don't share that experience... it's terrifying.

If you truly believed embracing certain parts of this mortal existence would cause eternal suffering, wouldn't you push away whatever might challenge that? If restricting your joy for several decades promised infinite bliss after (you literally get to become a god of your own worlds!), wouldn't it seem worth it?

If an expert in human psychology *confirmed* your fear that *gay thoughts* are maladies of the mind and temptations of the devil, and he has the solution, it's easy to overlook the wolf beneath the wool. When he rationalizes it is *normal* for things to worsen before getting better, you might incorrectly assume the signs of psychological abuse toward your child are the *worse before better*.

While twenty months were harmful enough, I am grateful I escaped it when I did. I accepted myself, or thought I had.

At the family meeting that Thanksgiving, when I told my family I was done with conversion therapy and would start living authentically, all but Jake took turns telling me they accepted my being gay, but they wouldn't accept me having a male partner. It wasn't much, but the needle moved. For a time, that was enough for me.

Jake's gesture of unconditional love—making my happiness his only metric for judgment—helped carry me through. It's funny, because when I set out to write this book, I didn't realize how significant that gesture was for me. It was my anchor to hope.

Over time, I challenged my family's various behaviors that the Family Acceptance Project calls "change efforts," as mentioned in chapter 1. These efforts included things like not asking about romance in my life and not being open to spending time with a partner or friends.

When I could, I also shared stories with them about the painful experiences my friends had with their own families because of their identities. These opened the door for them to have compassion for and be willing to hear more of their stories, about which my dad told me, "When they've been ostracized by their families or disowned, that's really hard to comprehend."

Like Black detailed in his memoir, I, too, "witnessed generations of my [family's] hand-me-down misconceptions be replaced with love, understanding, and acceptance" when they listened to my friends' stories of rejection and pain.[2] Through openness, curiosity, and courage, intolerance evolved into acceptance.

That didn't mean all their beliefs changed. Sure, they evolved to "You can have a gay relationship, but not one recognized by God and country." That was around when my dad gave the interview that received national attention and started a dialogue. It put a public spotlight on the discrepancies between the straight, gender-conforming majority, and LGBTQ+ humans.

As Plato described, that spotlight highlighted an opportunity "not only to ascend learning and to see the good but to be willing to descend again to those prisoners and to share their troubles and their honors, whether they are worth having or not."[3]

It required I swallow my pride, check my prejudice, and remember what it was like to see in the dark. Only then could I build a bridge by extending support for and acceptance of their incomplete evolution, as I explained to Anderson Cooper eleven years ago.

Through psychotherapy, I connected how traumatized I was from my journey and recognized my self-acceptance wasn't deep. I realized I accepted being queer was okay, but I hadn't fully embraced the diversity within me. For a while, I gaslit myself into believing conversion therapy helped me, but it didn't.

I *created* good out of my trauma. I *chose* to rise out of the ash—a phoenix, like the one tattooed on my right shoulder.

To do so, I had to pull meaning out of my trauma, turn pain into purpose, and leave the rest behind me.

Writing chapter 7 on my conversion trauma was quite challenging because my mind hid much of it from me, protecting me from the pain. It's bittersweet, but a lot of my life rests beneath the surface of my mind. It's deep enough I can't conjure it up but not deep enough to keep it from haunting me with whispered echoes: *I am an abomination, a deviant, unnatural, unlovable.*

I felt proud of Wendy when she told me about the advocacy she's done since her son came out, and I complimented her for quickly embracing him. She frowned and surprised me by telling me how uncomfortable it is to receive applause for being a "wonderful mother." Apparently, it happens quite often.

"I was just being a mother," Wendy said matter of factly. "This is what you do for your children. If he was straight, of course I'd be doing this. That isn't a testament of *Yay! I'm a good mom. Pat me on the back.* It's an indictment against society. Me showing up for and loving my child, like a mom is supposed to, is not doing anything special. I'm just loving him. The fact that is such a big deal, to me, is criminal."

Sadly, those of us who live with minority identities come to believe we are lucky—a unicorn—if we are seen and embraced fully. We are convinced we deserve less than the minimum and should gladly take whatever we are offered. Like Oliver Twist, we expect punishment and belittling simply for asking, "Please, sir, I want some more."[4]

A selection of us possess enough defiance and a sense of entitlement to recognize we deserve more and have the will to advocate for it. I'm grateful I am such a person.

When I expanded my capacity for self-compassion through psychotherapy, I decided acceptance wasn't enough. Acceptance was permission to exist. I deserved to have my identity celebrated the same way it would be if it aligned with the majority or *norm*.

I started challenging my family's acceptance, setting an expectation for more. They believed they accepted me, but I knew they could do better and raised the standard. I didn't cut them off or turn my back on them like many said I should. I made it clear they had room to evolve further.

I recognized they weren't alone in needing to. I had to evolve to embrace them fully and remember their eyes were not accustomed to the light of the sun—the light beyond the cave.

Once I did, I saw our common humanity, and they got to see me grow in my authenticity. Only then I realized, just like I wasn't to blame for the harms I experienced, neither were they. All of it was rooted in generational indoctrination and a tradition of squashing differences or calling them evil because they made groups in power uncomfortable.

It didn't dismiss or minimize my pain to absolve my family of the blame I assigned them early on. The time came to let go of blame and focus on the way forward.

Like my family and I evolved, we all can choose to embrace and celebrate difference. Diversity *is* the norm, my friends. We have all the resources we need because of our differences. Still, we question who deserves them.

We each can change the world if given the right opportunities to thrive. When you change the world for even one person, you've changed the world.

If you've learned anything from this book, I challenge you to take it further. Read the book again. You might pick out something new.

Remember, it's a journey toward the ideal. We won't get it right, a lot. That's how learning is supposed to happen.

Ask someone to share their story and really listen. Listen to learn more about something that piqued your curiosity, not to respond or relate with a story from your own life. Learn how others view life to see through their lens and build a more complete picture of the world. Be open to considering your beliefs aren't fully informed until you've done this work.

If you want to take it even further, share this book with people and tell them how it changed your life. You can also volunteer for or donate to human rights and social support organizations, be a mentor, and check the appendix for citations and resources.

Celebrate the differences you see in others. Our differences give us collective strength. They are not weaknesses.

The two most real and human things you can do to make change are to believe others' lived experiences and advocate for politicians and policies that celebrate diversity, not wipe it out.

Per John Stuart Mill, "Bad men need nothing more to compass their ends, than that good men should look on and do nothing… because he will not trouble himself to use his mind on the subject."[5]

Use your mind.

As more of us can truly see the world, more of us will be in a position to change it.

***

THE BEGINNING

Resources

Websites
Autistic Self-Advocacy Network
www.AutisticAdvocacy.org
Nonprofit organization run by and for autistic people, focusing on advocacy and services for the autistic community.

Born Perfect
www.BornPerfect.org
Nonprofit advocating to ban SOGIECE across the United States.

The Family Acceptance Project
www.FamilyProject.sfsu.edu
They have many resources for families with various cultural and religious backgrounds to prevent health risks, strengthen families, and build healthy futures for LGBTQ+ and gender-diverse children and youth.

The Gay and Lesbian Alliance Against Defamation
www.GLAAD.org
Media advocacy organization for LGBTQ+ issues, providing news and resources.

Gender Spectrum
www.GenderSpectrum.org
Gender Spectrum provides resources, training, and support for gender-inclusive environments, focusing on the needs and experiences of children and teenagers across the gender spectrum.

Human Rights Campaign
www.HRC.org
Advocacy organization for LGBTQ+ rights with a wide range of resources and reports.

Self-Compassion
www.Self-compassion.org
Resources for learning more about and practicing self-compassion and, in turn, foster more self- and other acceptance.

Neurodiversity Hub
www.NeurodiversityHub.org
Provides resources, insights, and support for understanding and embracing the spectrum of neurodiversity as natural variations in the human genome, advocating for appreciation and support of neurodivergent individuals.

Out Care
www.OutCareHealth.org
Working to revolutionize LGBTQ+ healthcare, providing trainings for providers and resources to find qualified health professionals near you.

Parents and Families of LGBTQ+
www.PFlag.org

Provides support, education, and advocacy for LGBTQ+ people, their families, and allies.

Psychology Today
www.PsychologyToday.com
Helps locate therapists with various specialties, including those experienced with LGBTQ+ issues.

Tara Brach—Radical Compassion Practice
www.TaraBrach.com/rain
Tara Brach's RAIN is a mindfulness tool that stands for recognize, allow, investigate, and nurture, used to manage difficult emotions and cultivate a compassionate, nonjudgmental awareness of oneself.

The Trevor Project
www.TheTrevorProject.org
Offers crisis support and advocates to end suicide among LGBTQ+ young people.

Books

The Art of Being Normal
by Lisa Williamson
A novel about two teenagers grappling with identity, friendship, and acceptance, with a focus on transgender experience.

The Autistic Brain: Helping Different Kinds of Minds Succeed
by Temple Grandin and Richard Panek
Temple Grandin, a renowned autistic author, provides personal insights combined with the latest research on the autistic brain.

Braving the Wilderness
by Brené Brown
Explores the journey to true belonging through authenticity, bravery, and standing up for what you believe in.

Daring Adventures: Helping Gender-Diverse Kids and Their Families Thrive
by Rachel A. Cornwell
As a reverend and the mother of a transgender child, she offers support and guidance for families who love their gender-diverse children.

Friendship Love Autism
by Michelle and Andrew Preston
A heartfelt account that delves into the dynamics of relationships and personal growth through the lens of autism, offering readers an intimate look at the challenges and triumphs faced by individuals on the spectrum. They also are great to follow on social media.
TikTok: @MichelleandAndrew
Instagram: @MichelleAndrewPreston

Gender Outlaw: On Men, Women, and the Rest of Us
by Kate Bornstein
A groundbreaking work on gender, breaking down traditional notions and offering a compelling narrative.

The Gifts of Imperfection
by Brené Brown
Encourages readers to embrace their imperfections and recognize their vulnerability as a source of courage, connection, and compassion.

How to Be an Antiracist
by Ibram X. Kendi
Provides a robust framework for understanding and dismantling racism and building an anti-racist society, emphasizing self-reflection and societal change.

Mama's Boy: A Story from Our Americas
by Dustin Lance Black
A memoir exploring his journey of identity, family, and activism within the context of his upbringing in a conservative Southern community.

Others
Alok V. Menon
TikTok, Instagram, Threads: @AlokVMenon
A queer poet, comedian, author, and activist.

Kat Blaque
YouTube: @KatBlaque
Transgender rights activist who discusses issues related to gender, race, and social justice.

Neurodivergent Rebel
NeurodivergentRebel.com
TikTok, Instagram, Threads: @NuerodivergentRebel
Queer and neurodivergent, explores autism and neurodiversity from an insider's perspective, advocating for acceptance and change.

About the Cover Illustration

Everything that happens to us in life is a matter of perspective and works to serve our growth. Whether it's a traumatic experience, a tough situation, or even the best of circumstances, we always have something to learn that serves us in wildly unexpected ways.

The same storm cloud that can topple houses also serves to water the crops that give us nourishment. In this way, nothing in life ever assumes a singular perspective.

The cover of this book serves to illustrate this exact point.

In the wake of a devastating lightning strike, the storm front and sunrise create a beautiful rainbow among the leaves of a tree of life. The tree provides shelter from the storm and symbolizes steady and consistent growth over time—a necessary ingredient for healing.

It's my hope this book serves to heal the hearts and minds of many, bringing families back together with love and compassion.

With love,
Ethan Starkey

Acknowledgments

As I pause at this juncture, reflecting on the myriad paths that have led to the completion of this book, my heart brims with gratitude. This book is not merely an anthology of my own musings. It is a vibrant mosaic, each piece a fragment of wisdom and love contributed by a diverse array of souls whose paths have intersected with mine. It's a testament to the power of collective wisdom and the beauty of learning from others, each perspective adding a unique hue to my understanding and shaping the narrative that unfolded—a beautiful rainbow of color.

Devon, your unrelenting optimism and love are my anchor. You are not only a pillar of support but also a mirror, revealing my blind spots and encouraging me to look at the world through a rose-colored lens. Your spirit helped carry me through when I doubted myself.

My beloved family, without you, I wouldn't have the resilience to carry on this work. Your love and support have sculpted the lens through which I view the world. Each of you has contributed to my evolving perspective, teaching me lessons of love, understanding, and growth that have been crucial in my journey. I hope my love for you is reflected in the words of this book and that you know I understand you always wanted the best for me.

My mom and dad: Nancy and Matt
My siblings and their partners: Lara and Matt, Jake and Sarah, Katie and Adam
My siblings' children: Jack, Grace, Charlotte, Sam, Travis, Annie, Dustin, Sofie, and Brigg

My amazing friends are the family I collected along this journey. To those who have traveled alongside me, sharing in the laughter and wisdom: You have been instrumental in broadening my horizon. You are by my side when I need you, whether for a shoulder to cry on, when I need advice, or to celebrate the joys of life. Each conversation and shared moment have added depth and color to my understanding, encouraging me to embrace a wider spectrum of thought and emotion in every line I pen.

A special shout out to my friend Ethan for the beautiful, original artwork on the cover he created specifically for this book.

And to every individual who contributed a thread to this intricate tapestry—colleagues, mentors, readers, and critics alike—your perspectives have been invaluable. You've challenged me to grow, give voice to the unheard, and weave each insight into a narrative I hope will guide others on their own paths toward embracing and celebrating the richness of life.

While embarking on the journey that lies within these pages, know that this work is a celebration of our shared humanity, a collective dream. It's a guide built on the foundation of courage and curiosity, aiming to inspire others to expand their perspectives and celebrate the breadth of human experience. With all the gratitude and hope I can muster, I thank you all for being the light and color in this bright prism.

To those vulnerable enough to share their personal journeys and expertise with me, I thank you:

Caitlin Ryan
Claudia Cardozo
Dustin Lance Black
Eric Wright
Leandra Stanley
Martha Lang

Michael Whitehouse
Neil Giuliano
Rachel Cornwell
Steve May
Wendy Williams Montgomery

For my community of early supporters who preordered and read early excerpts to give me feedback, your support helped make this book a reality.

Adriane Fugh-Berman
Alan Thompson
Alex Brewer
Alexa Tippets
Alicia Cowdrey
Andrew Ligon
Ann Kingston

Arin Lopez
Ashley Thorpe
Babak Hosseini
Bahney Dedolph
Ben Harris
Benjamin Brooks
Blake Larson

Blake Roberts
Bobby Parker
Brad Gudzinas
Brandy Reinke
Brian Garcia
Brian Keyser
Bronwyn Walsh
CJ Minott
Carlos Alfaro
Caryn Stone
Chris Huish
Christine Bink
Christine Glass
Christopher Hall
Colin Smith
Conrad Zeutenhorst
Crystal Ford
Dan Erickson
Daniel Taylor
Denton Shanks
Dion Foreman
Ella Mathews
Ethan Starkey
Evan Hale
Gabrielle Rush
Gary Brennan
Gene Sun
Heidi Rueda
Isaac Domingue
Jai Smith
Jania Davis
Jason Reynolds

Jason Schneider
Jess Yarbrough
Joseph Izzo
Kacie Birkmeyer
Kari Hamblin
Kasey Hegg
Kat Corzati
Keith Effertz
Kevin Smith
Kimberly Shill
Laurel Payne
Lenette Golding
Linda Elliott
Lindsay Howell
Luis Ramos
Luke Lukens
Marc Echeveste
Mark Szymanski
Matt Barker
Max Mayrink
Maya Heck
Melissa Harris
Molly Hart
Nathalie Szilagyi
Nate Rhoton
Nicole Gutierrez Miller
Nikki Rohner
Rebekah Richgels
Ross Francis
Samuel Edwards
Shannon Alexandra
Shannon Minter

Shannon Sesterhenn
Shawn Byers
Stella Kowalczyk
Stephanie Tyers
Tara Anderson

Taylor Wuerth
Tina Celenza Remillard
Tyler Allen
Tysen Schlink
William Lewallen

And finally, to the awesome team at Manuscripts LLC, without your tutelage and eye for revisions, this book wouldn't have become a reality.

Asa Loewenstein
Carol McKibben
Carolyn Farias
Clayton Bohle

Eric Koester
Jacques Moolman
Shanna Heath

Appendix

Introduction—Answering the Call

1. Kevin Cirilli, "Portman for Gay Marriage after Son Comes Out," *POLITICO*, March 15, 2013, https://www.politico.com/story/2013/03/rob-portman-gay-marriage-stance-088903.
2. Yahoo News, "Gay Son Doesn't Change Arizona Congressman's Position against Same-Sex Marriage," April 1, 2013, https://news.yahoo.com/blogs/ticket/arizona-congressman-gay-son-doesn-t-change-position-191347768--election.html.
3. "Conversion 'Therapy' Laws," Equality Maps, Movement Advancement Project, Accessed October 24, 2023, https://www.lgbtmap.org/equality-maps/conversion_therapy.
4. Raisa A. Rahim, "The Neuroevolutionary Roots of Xenophobia," *Explorations: The UC Davis Undergraduate Research Journal* Vol. 19 (December 21, 2017), http://Explorations.UCDavis.edu.
5. Ibid.
6. "Social Determinants of Health," Health Topics, World Health Organization, Accessed October 24, 2023, https://www.who.int/health-topics/social-determinants-of-health.

7. Thomas Jefferson et al., *US Declaration of Independence* (Philadelphia, PA: John Dunlap, 1776), 1.

Chapter 1—Family Assigned at Birth

1. Harper Lee, *To Kill a Mockingbird* (New York: Harper Perennial Modern Classics, 2006), 300.
2. Pew Research Center, *A Survey of LGBT Americans* (Washington, DC: Pew Research Center, 2013), 1.
3. Sabra L. Katz-Wise et al., "LGBT Youth and Family Acceptance," *Pediatric Clinics of North America* 63, no. 6 (December 2016): 1011–25, https://doi.org/10.1016/j.pcl.2016.07.005.
4. Diane N. Ruble et al., "The Role of Gender Constancy in Early Gender Development," *Child Development* 78, no. 4 (2007): 1121–36, https://doi.org/10.1111/j.1467-8624.2007.01056.x.
5. Janette Benson, ed., *Encyclopedia of Infant and Early Childhood Development (Second Edition)* (Oxford: Elsevier, 2020), 2:1–12.
6. Amit Paley, *2022 National Survey on LGBTQ Youth Mental Health* (New York: The Trevor Project, 2022), 4.
7. Leire Gartzia et al., "Emotional Androgyny: A Preventive Factor of Psychosocial Risks at Work?" *Frontiers in Psychology* 9, no. 2144 (November 2018): 1–18, https://doi.org/10.3389/fpsyg.2018.02144.
8. Sven Mueller, Griet de Cuypere, and Guy T'Sjoen, "Transgender Research in the 21st Century: A Selective Critical Review from a Neurocognitive Perspective," *The American Journal of Psychiatry* 174, no. 12 (October 2017): 1155–62, https://doi.org/10.1176/appi.ajp.2017.17060626.

9. Family Acceptance Project, "Families Matter!" Family Matters, LGBTQ Family Acceptance, Accessed October 31, 2023, https://lgbtqfamilyacceptance.org/family-matters/.
10. Brené Brown, *Daring Greatly: How the Courage to Be Vulnerable Transforms the Way We Live, Love, Parent, and Lead* (New York: Avery, 2012), 244–45.
11. Ibid.
12. Family Acceptance Project, "Families Matter!" Family Matters, LGBTQ Family Acceptance, Accessed October 31, 2023, https://lgbtqfamilyacceptance.org/family-matters/.
13. Brené Brown, *Daring Greatly: How the Courage to Be Vulnerable Transforms the Way We Live, Love, Parent, and Lead* (New York: Avery, 2012), 244–45.

Chapter 2—The Garden

1. Matthew 7:20 (KJV).
2. Zechariah 7:10 (KJV).
3. Matthew 25:40 (KJV).
4. John 13:34 (KJV).
5. Luke 12:48 (KJV).
6. Joseph Smith, *The Pearl of Great Price* (Salt Lake City, UT: The Church of Jesus Christ of Latter-day Saints, 2015), History 1:19.
7. James 1:5 (KJV).
8. Angie L. Dahl, and Renee V. Galliher, "LGBTQ Adolescents and Young Adults Raised within a Christian Religious Context: Positive and Negative Outcomes," *Journal of Adolescence* 35, no. 6 (December 2012): 1611–18, https://doi.org/10.1016/j.adolescence.2012.07.003.

9. Ibid.
10. Ibid.
11. 1 Corinthians 10:13 (KJV).
12. *Dictionary.com* (Oakland, California: Random House, 2023), s.v. "What Doesn't Kill You, Makes You Stronger," https://www.dictionary.com/e/slang/what-doesnt-kill-you-makes-you-stronger/.
13. Mark D. Seery, E. Alison Holman, and Roxane Cohen Silver, "Whatever Does Not Kill Us: Cumulative Lifetime Adversity, Vulnerability, and Resilience," *Journal of Personality and Social Psychology* 99, no. 6 (December 1, 2010): 1025–41, https://doi.org10.1037/a0021344.

Chapter 3—Pursuit of Happiness

1. Barry Goldwater, "Job Protection for Gays," *The Washington Post*, July 13, 1994.
2. Ibid.
3. Reince Priebus et al., *Republican Platform 2016* (Cleveland, OH: Consolidated Solutions, 2016), 9–11.
4. Thomas Jefferson et al., *US Declaration of Independence* (Philadelphia, PA: John Dunlap, 1776), 1.
5. James Madison et al., *Constitution of the United States* (Philadelphia, PA: Dunlap & Claypoole, 1787), 1–4.
6. Thomas Jefferson et al., *Declaration of Independence* (Philadelphia, PA: John Dunlap, 1776), 1.
7. Office of the Law Revision Counsel, *US Code, Title 5, Section 3331—Oath of Office* (Washington, DC: Government Printing Office, 2018), 242.
8. James Madison et al., *Constitution of the United States* (Philadelphia, PA: Dunlap & Claypoole, 1787), 1–4.

9. Gallup, Inc., "LGBTQ+ Rights," In-depth Topics A–Z, Gallup, accessed November 15, 2023, https://news.gallup.com/poll/1651/gay-lesbian-rights.aspx.
10. Reince Priebus et al., *Republican Platform 2016* (Cleveland, OH: Consolidated Solutions, 2016), 9–11.
11. NPR, "Loving Day: The 1967 Landmark Supreme Court Decision," June 2021, last modified June 12, 2022, https://www.npr.org/2021/06/12/1005848169/loving-day-interracial-marriage-legal-origin.
12. Reince Priebus et al., *Republican Platform 2016* (Cleveland, OH: Consolidated Solutions, 2016), 9–11.

Chapter 4—Monopoly

1. Chicago Associated Press, "King Berates Medical Care Given Negroes," *Oshkosh Northwestern*, March 26, 1966, https://www.newspapers.com/article/the-oshkosh-northwestern-oshkosh-daily-n/12049661/.
2. Commission on Social Determinants of Health, *Closing the gap in a Generation: Health Equity through Action on the Social Determinants of Health—Preface* (Switzerland: WHO Press, 2008).
3. Sarah O'Connor, "Left behind: Can Anyone Save the Towns the UK Economy Forgot?" *Financial Times*, November 16, 2017, https://www.ft.com/blackpool.
4. Latoya Hill, Samantha Artiga, and Usha Ranji, *Racial Disparities in Maternal and Infant Health: Current Status and Efforts to Address Them* (San Francisco: KFF, November 1, 2022).
5. Abraham Maslow, "A Theory of Human Motivation," *Psychological Review* 50, no. 4 (1943): 370–96, https://doi.org/10.1037/h0054346.

6. Louis Tay and Ed Diener, "Needs and Subjective Well-Being around the World," *Journal of Personality and Social Psychology* 101, no. 2 (2011), 354–65, https://doi.10.1037/a0023779.
7. Martha E. Lang and Chloe E. Bird, "Understanding and Addressing the Common Roots of Racial Health Disparities: The Case of Cardiovascular Disease and HIV/AIDS in African Americans," *Health Matrix: The Journal of Law-Medicine* 25, no. 1 (2015), 109–38, https://scholarlycommons.law.case.edu/healthmatrix/vol25/iss1/7.
8. Centre for Urban Health, *Social Determinants of Health: The Solid Facts*, eds. Richard Wilkinson and Michael Marmot (Copenhagen, Denmark: WHO Press, 1998), 1–27.
9. Commission on Social Determinants of Health, *Closing the Gap in a Generation: Health Equity through Action on the Social Determinants of Health* (Switzerland: WHO Press, 2008), 3.

Chapter 5—Neurofabulous

1. The Church of Jesus Christ of Latter-day Saints, "Lesson 27: The Age of Accountability," in *Primary 3* (Salt Lake City, UT: The Church of Jesus Christ of Latter-day Saints, 1994), 128–33.
2. 1 Corinthians 10:13 (KJV).
3. Cody Abramson, "What Causes Intrusive Thoughts?" *NOCD* (blog), March 23, 2023, https://www.treatmyocd.com/what-is-ocd/info/ocd-stats-and-science/what-causes-intrusive-thoughts.
4. Claire Henderson, Sara Evans-Lacko, and Graham Thornicroft, "Mental Illness Stigma, Help Seeking, and Public Health Programs," *American Journal of Public*

Health 103 (May 2023), 777–80, https://doi.org/10.2105/AJPH.2012.301056.
5. Patrick Corrigan, "Mental Health Stigma as Social Attribution: Implications for Research Methods and Attitude Change," *Clinical Psychology: Science and Practice* 7, no. 1 (May 2006), 48–67, https://doi.org/10.1093/clipsy.7.1.48.
6. Robert Austin and Gary Pisano, "Neurodiversity as a Competitive Advantage: Why You Should Embrace It in Your Workforce," *Harvard Business Review*, May/June 2017, 96–103, https://hbr.org/2017/05/neurodiversity-as-a-competitive-advantage.
7. Ibid.
8. Robert Austin and Gary Pisano, "Neurodiversity as a Competitive Advantage: Why You Should Embrace It in Your Workforce," *Harvard Business Review*, May/June 2017, 96–103, https://hbr.org/2017/05/neurodiversity-as-a-competitive-advantage.

Chapter 6—Wrestle with My Self-Loathing

1. Sven Mueller, Griet de Cuypere, and Guy T'Sjoen, "Transgender Research in the 21st Century: A Selective Critical Review from a Neurocognitive Perspective," *The American Journal of Psychiatry* 174, no. 12 (October 2017): 1155–1162, https://doi.org/10.1176/appi.ajp.2017.17060626.
2. Lih-Mei Liao et al., "Determinant Factors of Gender Identity: A Commentary," *Journal of Pediatric Urology* 8, no. 6 (November 2012): 597–601, https://doi.org/10.1016/j.jpurol.2012.09.009.

Chapter 7—Converting Two by Two

1. James 2:26 (KJV).
2. Mathew Shurka, "Mathew Shurka Forgives His Father After Enduring Years of Conversion Therapy," *I'm From Driftwood* (blog), *LGBTQIA+ Story Archive*, June 25, 2014, https://imfromdriftwood.com/story/mathew-shurka-forgives-his-father-after-enduring-years-of-conversion-therapy/.
3. Judith Glassgold and Caitlin Ryan, "The Role of Families in Efforts to Change, Support, and Affirm Sexual Orientation, Gender Identity and Expression in Children and Youth," in *The Case Against Conversion Therapy*, ed. Douglas Haldeman (Washington, DC: APA Books, 2022), 91.
4. United Nations, *Convention against Torture and Other Cruel, Inhuman or Degrading Treatment or Punishment* (Geneva, Switzerland: The Office of the High Commissioner for Human Rights, 1987), Article 1.
5. The Office of the High Commissioner for Human Rights, "'Conversion Therapy' Can Amount to Torture and Should Be Banned Says UN Expert," *United Nations Human Rights* (blog), July 13, 2020, https://www.ohchr.org/en/stories/2020/07/conversion-therapy-can-amount-torture-and-should-be-banned-says-un-expert.
6. Christy Mallory, Taylor Brown, and Kerith Conron, *Conversion Therapy and LGBT Youth* (Los Angeles, CA: UCLA School of Law Williams Institute, 2019), 1–5.
7. Movement Advancement Project, "Conversion Therapy Laws," *Equality Maps* (blog), accessed December 10, 2023, https://www.lgbtmap.org/equality-maps/conversion_therapy.

8. Governor Katie Hobbs, *Executive Order 2023-13: Protecting Young People from Conversion Therapy*" (Phoenix, Arizona: State of Arizona, 2023), 1–2.
9. Anna Forsythe, et al., "Humanistic and Economic Burden of Conversion Therapy Among LGBTQ Youths in the United States," *JAMA Pediatrics* 176, no. 5 (March 2022): 493–501. https://doi.org/10.1001/jamapediatrics.2022.0042.
10. Robert Hart, "Dangerous, Discredited' LGBTQ+ Conversion Therapy Costs US More Than $9 Billion Each Year, Study Finds," *Forbes*, March 8, 2022, https://www.forbes.com/sites/roberthart/2022/03/07/dangerous-discredited-lgbtq-conversion-therapy-costs-us-more-than-9-billion-each-year-study-finds.

Chapter 8—Finding Paradise

1. Brené Brown, *Braving the Wilderness: The Quest for True Belonging and the Courage to Stand Alone* (New York City, NY: Random House, 2017), 1–208.
2. Genesis 2:17 (KJV).
3. Genesis 1:28 (KJV).
4. Dustin Lance Black, *Mama's Boy: A Story from Our Americas* (New York City, NY: Knopf, 2019), 1–416.
5. Shelley Carson and Ellen Langer, "Mindfulness and Self-Acceptance," *Journal of Rational-Emotive & Cognitive-Behavior Therapy* 24, no. 1 (June 2006): 29–43, https://doi.org/10.1007/s10942-006-0022-5.
6. Ibid.
7. Shelley Carson and Ellen Langer, "Mindfulness and Self-Acceptance," *Journal of Rational-Emotive & Cognitive-Behavior Therapy* 24, no. 1 (June 2006): 29–43, https://doi.org/10.1007/s10942-006-0022-5.

8. Carl Rogers, *On Becoming a Person: A Therapist's View of Psychotherapy* (Boston, MA: Houghton Mifflin, 1961), 17.
9. Carl Rogers, *On Becoming a Person: A Therapist's View of Psychotherapy* (Boston, MA: Houghton Mifflin, 1961), 283–284.
10. Lady Gaga, "Getting to Know Lady Gaga" interview by Oprah Winfrey, *The Oprah Winfrey Show* (January 2010), https://www.oprah.com/oprahshow/lady-gagas-first-oprah-show-appearance/all.
11. Lady Gaga, "Lady Gaga: The Interview," interview by Derek Blasberg, *Harper's Bazar* (April 2011), https://www.harpersbazaar.com/celebrity/latest/news/a713/lady-gaga-interview/.
12. Justin Baldoni, Liz Plank, and Jamey Heath, "Alok Vaid-Menon: The Urgent Need for Compassion," *The Man Enough Podcast*, released July 26, 2021, 69:03, https://manenough.com/alok/.
13. RuPaul, "If you can't love yourself, how in the hell you gonna love somebody else? Can I get an amen?" X, February 4, 2013, https://x.com/rupaulsdragrace/status/298626899360505856?s=46&t=b5TobFAX7loVoyGGkssuxQ.

Chapter 9—Love Thy Neighbor

1. Matthew 22:37–39 (KJV).
2. Shelley Carson and Ellen Langer, "Mindfulness and Self-Acceptance," *Journal of Rational-Emotive & Cognitive-Behavior Therapy* 24, no. 1 (June 2006): 29–43, https://doi.org/10.1007/s10942-006-0022-5.
3. Kristin Neff, "Self-Compassion: An Alternative Conceptualization of a Healthy Attitude Toward

Oneself," *Self and Identity* 2 (2003): 96, https://doi.org/0.1080/15298860390129863.
4. Leandra Stanley, "Director of Diversity & Inclusion | DISM Certified—ISO 30415:2021 | Unapologetic, Fat, Black, Disabled, AuDHD, Neurodivergent, Queer, Polyam, Genderqueer | Work in Progress | NO SALES PITCHES, PLEASE," LinkedIn, Accessed December 27, 2023, https://www.linkedin.com/in/leandrastanley/.
5. Ipsos, *LGBT+ Pride 2021 Global Survey* (Paris, France: Ipsos, 2021), 4.
6. *Mama's Boy*, directed by Laurent Bouzerau (2022; HBO Documentary Films, 2022), 1:38:26, streamed on MAX.
7. Office of the US Surgeon General, *Our Epidemic of Loneliness and Isolation: The US Surgeon General's Advisory on the Healing Effects of Social Connection and Community* (Washington, DC: Public Health Reports 2023), 4–5.
8. Morning Consult, *The Loneliness Epidemic Persists: A Post-Pandemic Look at the State of Loneliness among US Adults* (Bloomfield, CT: The Cigna Group 2021).
9. Office of the US Surgeon General, *Our Epidemic of Loneliness and Isolation: The US Surgeon General's Advisory on the Healing Effects of Social Connection and Community* (Washington, DC: Public Health Reports 2023), 8.
10. Shelley Carson, and Ellen Langer, "Mindfulness and Self-Acceptance," *Journal of Rational-Emotive & Cognitive-Behavior Therapy* 24, no. 1 (June 2006): 29–43, https://doi.org/10.1007/s10942-006-0022-5.
11. Daryl Davis, "Why I, as a Black Man, Attend KKK Rallies," December 8, 2017, Naperville, IL, TEDx, 18:41, https://www.ted.com/talks/daryl_davis_why_i_as_a_black_man_attend_kkk_rallies.

Chapter 10—Returning to the Cave

1. John Stuart Mill, *Inaugural Address* (London: Longmans, Green, Reader, and Dyer, 1867), 74.
2. Micah Bazant, "Marsha P. Johnson," *Micah Bazant* (blog), Accessed January 3, 2024, https://www.micahbazant.com/#/marsha-p-johnson/.
3. Plato, "Book VII: On Shadows and Realities in Education," in *The Republic*, trans. Benjamin Jowett (New York, NY: Colonial Press, 1901), 209–216, http://www.its.caltech.edu/~haugen/Plato-Republic-Jowett.pdf.
4. Ibid.
5. *Mama's Boy*, directed by Laurent Bouzerau (2022; HBO Documentary Films, 2022), 1:01:34, streamed on MAX.
6. The United States Supreme Court, *Obergefell v. Hodges*, *135 S.Ct. 2584* (Washington, DC: United States Reports, 2015), 13.
7. American Civil Liberties Union, "Mapping Attacks on LGBTQ Rights in US State Legislatures," Legislative Attacks on LGBTQ Rights, ACLU, last modified December 21, 2023, https://www.aclu.org/legislative-attacks-on-lgbtq-rights.
8. The United States Supreme Court, *Obergefell v. Hodges*, *135 S.Ct. 2584* (Washington, DC: United States Reports, 2015), 19.
9. Vivek Murthy, *Our Epidemic of Loneliness and Isolation: The US Surgeon General's Advisory on the Healing Effects of Social Connection and Community* (Washington, DC: Office of the US Surgeon General, 2023), 4.

Conclusion—Embracing the Journey

1. Dustin Lance Black, *Mama's Boy* (New York, NY: Knopf Doubleday Publishing Group, 2018) chapter 23, Kindle.
2. Ibid., chapter 17, Kindle.
3. Plato, "Book VII: On Shadows and Realities in Education," in *The Republic*, trans. Benjamin Jowett (New York, NY: Colonial Press, 1901), 209–216, http://www.its.caltech.edu/~haugen/Plato-Republic-Jowett.pdf.
4. Charles Dickens, *Oliver Twist* (New York, NY: James G. Gregory, 1861), 34.
5. John Stuart Mill, *Inaugural Address* (London: Longmans, Green, Reader, and Dyer, 1867), 74.

Made in the USA
Middletown, DE
15 May 2024